LOUIS B. WRIGHT, General Editor. Director of the Folger Shakespeare Library from 1948 until his retirement in 1968, Dr. Wright has devoted over forty years to the study of the Shakespearean period. In 1926 he completed his doctoral thesis on "Vaudeville Elements in Elizabethan Drama" and subsequently published many articles on the stagecraft and theatre of Shakespeare's day. He is the author of *Middle-Class Culture in Elizabethan England* (1935), *Religion and Empire* (1942), *The Elizabethans' America* (1965), and many other books and essays on the history and literature of the Tudor and Stuart periods, including *Shakespeare for Everyman* (1964). Dr. Wright has taught at the universities of North Carolina, California at Los Angeles, Michigan, Minnesota, and other American institutions. From 1932 to 1948 he was instrumental in developing the research program of the Henry E. Huntington Library and Art Gallery. During his tenure as Director, the Folger Shakespeare Library became one of the leading research institutions of the world for the study of the backgrounds of Anglo-American civilization.

VIRGINIA A. LaMAR, Assistant Editor. A member of the staff of the Folger Shakespeare Library from 1946 until her death in 1968, Miss LaMar served as research assistant to the Director and as Executive Secretary. Prior to 1946 Miss LaMar had been a secretary in the British Admiralty Delegation in Washington, D.C., receiving the King's Medal in 1945 for her services. She was coeditor of the *Historie of Travell into Virginia Britania* by William Strachey, published by The Hakluyt Society in 1953, and author of *English Dress in the Age of Shakespeare* and *Travel and Roads in England* in the "Folger Booklets on Tudor and Stuart Civilization" series.

Ben Jonson.
Mezzotint after Gerard van Honthorst (n.d.)

Folger Print collection

VOLPONE

By
Ben Jonson

Edited with an Introduction by
Louis B. Wright and Virginia A. LaMar,
Folger Shakespeare Library.

WSP
WASHINGTON SQUARE PRESS · NEW YORK

VOLPONE

Washington Square Press edition published April, 1970

L

Published by Washington Square Press,
a division of Simon & Schuster, Inc., 630 Fifth Avenue, New York, N.Y.

WASHINGTON SQUARE PRESS editions are distributed in the
U.S. by Simon & Schuster, Inc., 630 Fifth Avenue, New
York, N.Y. 10020 and in Canada by Simon & Schuster
of Canada, Ltd., Richmond Hill, Ontario, Canada.

Standard Book Number: 671-45744-6.

Ben Jonson and *Volpone*

Ben Jonson, the friend of Shakespeare and the idol of a school of writers who styled themselves "the tribe of Ben," was the most learned of the Elizabethan playwrights—and one of the most vain.

Jonson was born in 1572 at Westminster, the son of a minister of Scottish background whose name is unknown. Shortly after his father's death his mother married a bricklayer. His name, too, is unknown. Through the intervention of a friend, believed traditionally to have been the antiquarian, William Camden, then headmaster of Westminster School, Ben was admitted to the school and there received the foundation of the classical learning for which he became noted. Apparently he was destined for Cambridge, as were many Westminster boys, but something interfered and he was put to his stepfather's craft of bricklaying, much to his disgust. Leaving his trade, he joined the English army in Flanders and killed an enemy in single combat. Sometime between 1592 and 1596 Jonson married, but we know little about his wife except that her husband later reported that she was "a shrew, but honest." She and her husband were haled before a Consistory Court in 1606 for failure to attend church. The couple had a daughter and two sons; two died in childhood and one son died two years before his father's own death, which occurred in 1637.

By 1597 Ben Jonson was in the employ of Philip Henslowe as a playwright. Writing for the stage was the best means that an ambitious young intellectual could take if he proposed to live by his pen, and

Jonson had a living to make. For the next forty years he was an industrious man of letters. For a time, early in his career, he was an actor—and gossips said a bad actor. He apparently was one of the performers of *The Isle of Dogs,* which incurred the wrath of the authorities, who suppressed it on July 28, 1597, jailed the cast, and closed all the theatres. There is a record of Jonson's release from prison, along with two other actors, in the following October. This was the first of several brushes with the law that Ben Jonson was to suffer. From the time of his release until 1602 he was writing at intervals for Henslowe, but he took time out to supply Shakespeare's company with plays and to write for the Children of the Chapel Royal when they were playing at the Blackfriars in 1600.

After a quarrel with Gabriel Spencer, one of Henslowe's leading actors, Jonson challenged him to a duel and killed him on September 22, 1598, an event that very nearly brought him to the gallows, but by pleading benefit of clergy he saved his neck. "Benefit of clergy" was a curious survival in English law that allowed anyone who could read the first verse of the Fifty-First Psalm to claim to be an ecclesiastical "clerk" and hence subject only to ecclesiastical courts for trial for certain crimes.

During the years 1600 to 1602 Jonson was engaged in the controversy between rival playwrights that is known as the "war of the theatres," and his pen was mainly devoted to satirical jibes at John Marston and other rivals. In 1605 he wrote a court masque that won favorable attention, and between that date and 1612 he wrote seven more highly successful masques for performance at court. Inigo Jones was the architect and designer responsible for mounting the masques. These entertainments, a mixture of pageantry, music, dancing, and spectacle, were extremely popular at the Jacobean court, and Jonson's skill in producing scripts proved financially profitable to him.

In the autumn of 1612 Jonson went to France as the tutor to Sir Walter Raleigh's son Wat, who, he reported, was "knavishly inclined." At any rate, young Raleigh took advantage of the drunkenness of his tutor to place him on a sledge and drag him through the principal streets of Paris with his arms crossed as a sign of his conversion to the Catholic faith—a conversion that did not last out his life. Jonson returned to London in 1613 and resumed his literary labors.

His reputation as a writer of masques and entertainments was already established; he was admired as a writer of both lyrical and satirical verse; and at intervals he continued to produce plays for the professional stage.

Late in the winter of 1618 Jonson made a visit to Scotland and was given a cordial reception by the literati of Edinburgh. During the following January he visited the Scottish poet, William Drummond of Hawthornden, and delivered himself of an amusing flow of information and opinions that have been published as *Ben Jonson's Conversations with William Drummond of Hawthornden*. In the July after his return from Scotland, Jonson visited Oxford and had conferred upon him in Convocation the honorary degree of Master of Arts—a singular honor for a man who had never darkened the doors of either university. He enjoyed a pension of one hundred marks a year, granted by King James, and was that sovereign's favorite man of letters. With the accession of King Charles I in 1625 new favorites won court favor, and Jonson was called upon less often for entertainments. In 1628, however, he received an appointment as "chronologer" or city historian of London, a post that helped him financially. It was said that the city fathers hoped to soften his sharp jibes at merchants and tradesmen by giving him this sop.

After several years of illness Jonson died at Westminster in 1637 and was buried in Westminster Abbey. A blue flagstone over his grave was inscribed with the simple phrase "O rare Ben Jonson!" For years he had been the most honored member of the writing profession; in the year after his death his literary friends produced a volume of elegiac verses entitled *Jonsonus Virbius*.

As a dramatist, Jonson was at his best when he could loose the arrows of his satirical wit at some target worthy of his attack. He lacked the range of a Shakespeare or the untrammeled imagination of a Marlowe, but at lashing the follies and foibles of mankind none could surpass him. It has been said, perhaps unfairly, that Jonson believed that the world was composed chiefly of fools and knaves and that the knaves had the better of it. Certainly we find in Jonson's comedies a great assembly of both fools and knaves, and he flogs them both without mercy. He believed profoundly that the comic dramatist had a duty to rebuke man for his follies.

Ben Jonson, like the great Dr. Johnson of the eighteenth century, spoke with the voice of common sense and expressed his disdain of sham, humbuggery, and pretentiousness with a vigor that few could match. The London of his day offered a fertile field for the satirist, and Jonson's keen eye missed nothing. London teemed with "projectors"—familiar to us as "promoters"—and Jonson found them particularly suitable for his ridicule. Fops, dandies, rascals, frauds of sundry sorts, rogues of every variety, pretenders to learning, pious hypocrites, social climbers, pompous parvenus, and a host of other undesirable characters found their way into his comedies of manners. Jonson caught their characteristics and portrayed them in words as vividly as Hogarth later was to picture them on canvas.

Although Jonson was the most learned of the dramatists of his time in classical lore, his comedies, even when based on Latin sources and given a foreign setting, are comedies of manners reflecting situations in London. His first great success in this vein was *Every Man in His Humor* (1598), which he initially gave a Venetian setting with Latin and Italian names for his characters, but he later revised the play and made it purely English. Shakespeare was one of the comedians who played in *Every Man in His Humor*. Jonson followed this play with *Every Man Out of His Humor* (1599), *Cynthia's Revels* (1601), *The Poetaster* (1601), *Sejanus* (1603), a classical tragedy that offended the authorities, and *Eastward Ho!* (1605), a comedy written in collaboration with George Chapman and John Marston, which satirized the Scots and so offended the King's favorites that the authors were thrown into prison for a time. The play that followed this experience was *Volpone* (1606).

In this play Jonson gave full rein to the satirical portrayal of types of characters recognizable in Jacobean London, though Mosca the parasite and his master Volpone were stock types in Roman comedy. Someone has commented that it is important to understand Jonson's sources, which are commonly in books rather than in observations made from life, and that *Volpone* is a mosaic made up from suggestions found in many classical works. But this view does Jonson less than justice, for, learned as he was, he was not pedantic in the use of source material, which he adapted to situations in real life.

For *Volpone* Jonson obtained ideas and plot elements from various writers—Lucian, Plutarch, Petronius, Diogenes Laertius, and Erasmus' *Praise of Folly*—but he digested his material thoroughly and made it completely his own. We are not conscious of any "mosaic" effect. This play is a clearly organized and brilliant presentation of a gallery of rogues, who move inevitably to their own destruction.

Critics have objected that Jonson is at his best when dealing with rascals and is never very successful in trying to portray a noble character. For example, when he attempts to characterize women he succeeds brilliantly with Lady Politic Wouldbe but makes the virtuous Celia a colorless piece of cardboard. In Jonson one will look in vain for the charming and gracious women who people Shakespeare's plays. Jonson was not at home with such personalities as Shakespeare's Rosalind and Portia. His appeal was always to the mind and not the heart, and his most notable dramatic successes were satires in which he showed the retribution that overtook the dupes of chicanery and knavery. *Volpone* is one of the greatest plays of this type.

For the modern reader or theatre-goer, *Volpone* is the most satisfactory of Jonson's plays, for it deals with a subject of universal interest—greed—and it depends less upon topical allusions and conditions peculiar to the London of the author's day than do his comedies of manners. Although Jonson utilized situations common in the Roman satirists, and the play is filled with classical allusions, the author's own learning in this play does not obtrude and become burdensome. Indeed, his learning is so thoroughly digested, assimilated, and adapted to the times that one is scarcely aware of the play's classical background.

One should also remember that *Volpone* was

written for performance before a popular audience at the Globe, though later the play proved an equally successful piece for presentation at court, and it remained a favorite for generations to come. Jonson was careful to indicate to the spectators that his story not only derived from classical sources but also drew upon beast fables as well. The names of several of the characters come straight from the bestiaries. Volpone means fox; Voltore, vulture; Corbaccio, crow; Corvino, raven; and Mosca, fly. Lest any unlearned member of the audience fail to recognize the names, here and there in the text, the author translates them into English in casual allusions to them.

The legend of the fox who feigned death was common in folklore and was handed down by word of mouth. Beast fables, of course, from Aesop onwards had been among the most widely circulated forms of story. All through the Middle Ages and the Renaissance, stories of animals with human attributes were common. The tale of Reynard the Fox was perhaps the most widely circulated of all, and to the fox was attributed a sly cunning that manifested itself in many ways. It was natural, therefore, for Jonson to choose Volpone the Fox for a character that embodied the ultimate in sly cunning.

Volpone is more than a mere satire on human greed, though it is that too. It goes beyond the concept of greed to provide a satiric commentary on the fascination with wealth that affects all of mankind, and the power of wealth to corrupt. That is the theme that runs through the whole play. Old Volpone is not a mere miser who piles up gold and other treasure for its own sake; he himself is also the fascinated observer of the power that the dream of wealth exerts upon others. He delights not merely in bilking greedy individuals of their wealth, but he also gets pleasure from contemplating their morbid concern with the acquisition of gold, with the ends to which they will go to enrich themselves. For an interval the voluptuary in Volpone may make him lust after Celia, but an even deeper emotion is his desire to watch Corvino demean himself by offering to sacrifice his wife's honor to have himself named the Fox's heir. Shakespeare in a famous passage had made Falstaff describe honor as "air." Jonson echoes him in having Corvino reply to his wife's agonizing debate by this dismissal of honor:

> Honor! Tut, a breath;
> There's no such thing in nature: a mere term
> Invented to awe fools. What is my gold
> The worse for touching? Clothes for being
>   looked on?   [III, ii, ll. 311–314]

So, having convinced himself that the hope of gain was of greater value than the honor of a virtuous wife, he orders Celia to go to bed with the old man.

Volpone does little to disprove the charge that Jonson regarded the world as filled with fools and knaves, but in this case, the knaves in the end receive the justice that they richly deserve. The play holds its suspense to the very end and the audience has few clues to the solution in which Volpone, Mosca, and the lesser rascals are revealed for what they are. Jonson in this play displayed an unusual sense of the requirements of the theatre, and that theatrical quality has insured the longevity of this play above any others that he wrote.

Elizabethan and Jacobean plays characteristically had a subplot, and Jonson conformed to convention by supplying the characters of Sir Politic Wouldbe, his garrulous lady, and Peregrine in a few rather loosely connected satirical episodes. Some scholars

have thought that Jonson was satirizing a particular
individual recognizable in London in his time in the
character of Sir Politic, but in view of the trouble
earlier encountered by Jonson because of supposed
topical allusions in plays, that would seem doubtful.
He is not likely to have run that risk in *Volpone*,
and no one at the time accused him of meddling
with recognizable political figures on the English
scene.

Sir Politic Wouldbe, however, is a character always with us and we can discern similarities between him and contemporaries today. For Sir
Politic is one who can always smell out a spy or a
seditious person at every turn. Concerning one of
these, he comments:

> I knew him one of the most dangerous heads
> Living within the state, and so I held him.

       *   *   *

> He has received weekly intelligence,
> Upon my knowledge, out of the Low Countries,
> For all parts of the world, in cabbages;
> And those dispensed again t'ambassadors,
> In oranges, muskmelons, apricots,
> Lemons, pomecitrons, and suchlike; sometimes
> In Colchester oysters and your Selsey cockles.

       *   *   *

>   Sir, upon my knowledge.
> Nay, I have observed him, at your public
>   ordinary,
> Take his advertisement from a traveler—
> A concealed statesman—in a trencher of meat;
> And instantly, before the meal was done,
> Convey an answer in a toothpick.

                        [II, i, ll. 89–104]

Thus, despite its antique dress, *Volpone* has a universality and a modernity that makes it a living play for us. The revelation of human frailties may not make it a cheery comedy, but it remains a funny one. Jonson himself was a witty man and he gives his wit full rein in *Volpone*.

In several plays after the production of *Volpone* Jonson continued his satire of the manners and mores of his own age and milieu; as elsewhere, he utilized characterizations and plot situations familiar from Roman comedy, but he naturalized them in London. In *Epicoene; or, The Silent Woman* (1609) he created a farce ridiculing the garrulity of women, city fops and gulls, and the pretensions of pseudo-learned women. In *The Alchemist* (1610) he wrote one of his greatest comedies of manners, presenting a vast array of cheats of the type that infested London at the time: alchemists, astrologers, fortune-tellers, fortune hunters, and a host of other rogues. This play displays not only the classical learning for which Jonson was noted but his familiarity with the terminology of the pseudo-science of his own time. In *Bartholomew Fair* (1614), the dramatist produced another array of dupes, rogues, and hypocrites familiar to Londoners, including a character named Zeal-in-the-Land Busy, a type of psalm-singing Puritan particularly detested by Jonson.

Jonson's comedies, filled as they are with farcical situations, are more than mere amusing entertainments. The dramatist conceived of comedy as a means of correcting the faults of mankind and of himself as the chosen instrument to punish folly and rascality wherever he observed it.

Jonson had a high opinion of his own literary production. In 1616 he supervised the publication of a folio edition of his collected plays, which he entitled *The Works of Benjamin Jonson*. The public had not previously considered plays written for the common theatres worthy of being considered "works," and Jonson's enemies ridiculed him for colossal vanity. Time, however, has accepted his literary judgment as sound.

The text of *Volpone* printed here is based on that in the 1616 folio edition of Jonson's works. Although the play was first printed in quarto form in 1607, the folio text must be considered more authoritative, since Jonson himself saw the volume through the press and was responsible for many small changes in phraseology.

Volpone was popular in Jonson's own time and has delighted audiences since. It was performed at the Globe early in 1606 and at both universities. It had a court performance in 1624 and was revived several times during the reign of Charles I. It was one of the Elizabethan plays that the Restoration found pleasing. Samuel Pepys saw it on January 14, 1665, and declared it "a most excellent play, the best I ever saw, and well acted." *Volpone* was frequently performed throughout the eighteenth century, but the nineteenth century found its satire not to its liking. A critic in 1816 declared that his was an "age of dramatic imbecility" that preferred spectacle instead of good drama, and in this atmosphere Jonson's play went into eclipse. In the twentieth century it has had many revivals on the public as well as the academic stages. Adaptations by Ludwig Tieck, Emile Zola, and Stefan Zweig (in collaboration with Jules Romains) indicate the appeal that Jonson's play has had for foreign critics and writers. The Zweig adaptation has little relation to the original, but it has had a considerable stage popularity recently.

[DEDICATORY EPISTLE]

To the most noble and most equal sisters, the two famous universities, for their love and acceptance shown to his poem in the presentation, Ben Jonson, the grateful acknowledger, dedicates both it and himself. 5

Never, most equal sisters, had any man a wit so presently excellent as that it could raise itself but there must come both matter, occasion, commenders, and favorers to it. If this be true, and that the fortune of all writers doth daily prove it, it behooves the care- 10
ful to provide well toward these accidents, and, having acquired them, to preserve that part of reputation most tenderly wherein the benefit of a friend is also defended. Hence it is that I now render myself grateful and am studious to justify the bounty of your act, 15
to which, though your mere authority were satisfying, yet, it being an age wherein poetry and the professors of it hear so ill on all sides, there will a reason be looked for in the subject. It is certain, nor can it with any forehead be opposed, that the too much license 20
of poetasters in this time hath much deformed their mistress, that every day their manifold and manifest ignorance doth stick unnatural reproaches upon her. But for their petulancy it were an act of the greatest injustice either to let the learned suffer or so divine 25
a skill, which indeed should not be attempted with

(Epistle)
2. UNIVERSITIES: Oxford and Cambridge.
11. ACCIDENTS: happenings.
18. HEAR SO ILL: hear themselves so ill spoken of.
20. FOREHEAD: boldness.
21. POETASTERS: rhymesters.
22. MISTRESS: the Muse of poetry.

---

unclean hands, to fall under the least contempt. For
if men will impartially and not asquint look toward
the offices and function of a poet, they will easily
conclude to themselves the impossibility of any man's   30
being the good poet without first being a good man.
He that is said to be able to inform young men to all
good disciplines, inflame grown men to all great virtues, keep old men in their best and supreme state,
or, as they decline to childhood, recover them to their   35
first strength; that comes forth the interpreter and
arbiter of nature, a teacher of things divine no less
than human, a master in manners; and can alone, or
with a few, effect the business of mankind—this, I take
him, is no subject for pride and ignorance to exercise   40
their railing rhetoric upon. But it will here be hastily
answered that the writers of these days are other
things; that not only their manners but their natures
are inverted and nothing remaining with them of the
dignity of poet but the abused name, which every   45
scribe usurps; that now, especially in dramatic or, as
they term it, stage poetry, nothing but ribaldry, prof-
anation, blasphemy, all license of offense to God
and man is practiced. I dare not deny a great part of
this, and am sorry I dare not, because in some men's   50
abortive features (and would they had never boasted
the light) it is overtrue; but that all are embarked in
this bold adventure for hell is a most uncharitable
thought and, uttered, a more malicious slander. For
my particular, I can, and from a most clear conscience, 55

32. INFORM: shape.
55. PARTICULAR: own self.
59. SCENE: stage.
63. POLITICS: schemers; troublemakers.
67. ALLOWED: licensed (i.e., not censored as were some of his col-
laborative plays).
75. ENTITLE: earn the credit for.
77. CARRIED: handled; OBNOXIOUS: liable.
77-78. CONSTRUCTION: interpretation.
78. MARRY: indeed.
79. APPLICATION: interpretation in terms of personalities.
87. RAKED UP: buried.
90. INTRENCH: gash; STYLES: pun on a form of the word "stylus."
92. GRAVED: buried.

affirm that I have ever trembled to think toward the
least profaneness, have loathed the use of such foul
and unwashed bawdry as is now made the food of the
scene; and, howsoever I cannot escape from some
the imputation of sharpness but that they will say I 60
have taken a pride or lust to be bitter, and not my
youngest infant but hath come into the world with
all his teeth, I would ask of these supercilious politics
what nation, society, or general order or state I have
provoked; what public person; whether I have not in 65
all these preserved their dignity, as mine own person,
safe. My works are read, allowed (I speak of those
that are entirely mine); look into them. What broad
reproofs have I used? Where have I been particular,
where personal, except to a mimic, cheater, bawd, or 70
buffoon—creatures for their insolencies worthy to be
taxed? Yet to which of these so pointingly as he might
not either ingenuously have confessed or wisely dis-
sembled his disease? But it is not rumor can make
men guilty, much less entitle me to other men's 75
crimes. I know that nothing can be so innocently writ
or carried but may be made obnoxious to construction; marry, whilst I bear mine innocence about me,
I fear it not. Application is now grown a trade with
many; and there are that profess to have a key for the 80
deciphering of everything. But let wise and noble
persons take heed how they be too credulous or give
leave to these invading interpreters to be overfamiliar
with their fames, who cunningly and often utter their
own virulent malice under other men's simplest mean- 85
ings. As for those that will (by faults which charity
hath raked up or common honesty concealed) make
themselves a name with the multitude, or, to draw
their rude and beastly claps, care not whose living
faces they intrench with their petulant styles, may 90
they do it without a rival for me! I choose rather to
live graved in obscurity than share with them in so

preposterous a fame. Nor can I blame the wishes of
those severe and wiser patriots, who, providing the
hurts these licentious spirits may do in a state, desire   95
rather to see fools and devils and those antique relics
of barbarism retrieved, with all other ridiculous and
exploded follies, than behold the wounds of private
men, of princes and nations, for, as Horace makes
Trebatius speak among these,   100

   Sibi quisque timet, quanquam est intactus, et odit.

And men may justly impute such rages, if continued, to the writer as his sports. The increase of which
lust in liberty, together with the present trade of the
stage in all their misc'line interludes, what learned   105
or liberal soul doth not already abhor? where nothing
but the filth of the time is uttered, and that with such
impropriety of phrase, such plenty of solecisms, such
dearth of sense, so bold prolepses, so racked meta-
phors, with brothelry able to violate the ear of a   110
pagan and blasphemy to turn the blood of a Christian
to water. I cannot but be serious in a cause of this
nature, wherein my fame and the reputations of divers
honest and learned are the question; when a name so
full of authority, antiquity, and all great mark is   115
through their insolence become the lowest scorn of
the age and those men subject to the petulancy of
every vernaculous orator that were wont to be the
care of kings and happiest monarchs. This it is that

---

93. PREPOSTEROUS: reversed in order (earned not by merit but by
attacking that of others).
94. PROVIDING: foreseeing.
98. EXPLODED: driven away (from the stage) with hoots.
101. SIBI . . . ODIT: Horace, *Satires*, ii.1.23. "Everyone is afraid for
himself, though untouched, and hates you."
105. MISC'LINE INTERLUDES: mixed entertainments.
109. PROLEPSES: anachronisms.
118. VERNACULOUS: scurrilous.
126. REDUCE: bring back.
130. CATASTROPHE: final scene (of the play).
133-34. OF INDUSTRY: intentionally.
140-41. GOINGS OUT: endings.
155-56. PRIMITIVE: original.

hath not only rapt me to present indignation but made 120
me studious heretofore, and, by all my actions, to
stand off from them, which may most appear in this
my latest work, which you, most learned arbitresses,
have seen, judged, and to my crown approved, wherein I have labored for their instruction and amendment 125
to reduce not only the ancient forms but manners of
the scene, the easiness, the propriety, the innocence,
and, last, the doctrine, which is the principal end of
poesy, to inform men in the best reason of living. And
though my catastrophe may, in the strict rigor of 130
comic law, meet with censure, as turning back to my
promise, I desire the learned and charitable critic to
have so much faith in me to think it was done of industry, for with what ease I could have varied it nearer his scale (but that I fear to boast my own faculty) 135
I could here insert. But my special aim being to put
the snaffle in their mouths that cry out, "We never
punish vice in our interludes," etc., I took the more
liberty, though not without some lines of example,
drawn even in the ancients themselves, the goings 140
out of whose comedies are not always joyful, but ofttimes the bawds, the servants, the rivals, yea, and the
masters are mulcted—and fitly, it being the office of a
comic poet to imitate justice and instruct to life as
well as purity of language, or stir up gentle affections, 145
to which I shall take the occasion elsewhere to speak.

For the present, most reverenced sisters, as I have
cared to be thankful for your affections past and
here made the understanding acquainted with some
ground of your favors, let me not despair their con- 150
tinuance to the maturing of some worthier fruits,
wherein, if my Muses be true to me, I shall raise the
despised head of Poetry again and, stripping her out
of those rotten and base rags wherewith the times
have adulterated her form, restore her to her primi- 155
tive habit, feature, and majesty, and render her wor-

thy to be embraced and kissed of all the great and
master spirits of our world. As for the vile and sloth-
ful, who never affected an act worthy of celebration,
or are so inward with their own vicious natures as 160
they worthily fear her and think it a high point of
policy to keep her in contempt with their declama-
tory and windy invectives, she shall out of just rage
incite her servants (who are *genus irritabile*) to spout
ink in their faces, that shall eat farther than their mar- 165
row, into their fames; and not Cinnamus the barber
with his art shall be able to take out the brands, but
they shall live and be read till the wretches die, as
things worst deserving of themselves in chief and then
of all mankind. 170

---

160. INWARD: familiar.
164. GENUS IRRITABILE: the touchy tribe (of poets) (Horace *Epistles* ii.2.102).
166. CINNAMUS: a barber-surgeon in one of the satires of Martial.

The Persons of the Play

Volpone, a magnifico.
Mosca, his parasite.
Voltore, an advocate.
Corbaccio, an old gentleman.
Corvino, a merchant.
Avocatori, four magistrates.
Notario, the register.
Nano, a dwarf.
Castrone, an eunuch.
Grege [the Mob].
[Sir] *Politic Wouldbe,* a knight.
Peregrine, a gentleman-traveler.
Bonario, a young gentleman.
Fine Madam Wouldbe, the knight's wife.
Celia, the merchant's wife.
Commandadori, officers.
Mercatori, three merchants.
Androgyno, a hermaphrodite.
Servitore, a servant.
Women [servants].

THE SCENE: *Venice.*

Mountebank scene from an eighteenth-century performance of the play.

From [Ben Jonson], *Volpone, or the Fox* (1732).

THE ARGUMENT

V olpone, childless, rich, feigns sick, despairs;
O ffers his state to hopes of several heirs;
L ies languishing. His parasite receives
P resents of all, assures, deludes, then weaves
O ther cross plots, which ope themselves, are told.   5
N ew tricks for safety are sought; they thrive; when, bold,
E ach tempts the other again, and all are sold.

PROLOGUE

Now luck God send us, and a little wit
   Will serve to make our play hit;
According to the palates of the season,
   Here is rhyme not empty of reason.
This we were bid to credit from our poet,   5
   Whose true scope, if you would know it,
In all his poems still hath been this measure,
   To mix profit with your pleasure;
And not as some whose throats, their envy failing,
   Cry hoarsely, "All he writes is railing";   10
And, when his plays come forth, think they can flout them
   With saying he was a year about them.
To these there needs no lie but this his creature,
   Which was two months since no feature;   15
And though he dares give them five lives to mend it,
   'Tis known, five weeks fully penned it,
From his own hand, without a coadjutor,

(Argument)
7. SOLD: cheated.

(Prologue)
7. STILL: ever.
8. PROFIT . . . PLEASURE: the prescription for poetry according to Horace's *Ars poetica*.
18. COADJUTOR: assistant.

Novice, journeyman, or tutor.
Yet thus much I can give you as a token   20
  Of his play's worth: no eggs are broken,
Nor quaking custards with fierce teeth affrighted,
  Wherewith your rout are so delighted;
Nor hales he in a gull, old ends reciting,
  To stop gaps in his loose writing;   25
With such a deal of monstrous and forced action,
  As might make Bedlam a faction.
Nor made he his play for jests stol'n from each table,
  But makes jests to fit his fable;
And so presents quick comedy, refined   30
  As best critics have designed.
The laws of time, place, persons he observeth;
  From no needful rule he swerveth.
All gall and copperas from his ink he draineth;
  Only a little salt remaineth,   35
Wherewith he'll rub your cheeks till, red with
    laughter,
They shall look fresh a week after.

---

22. QUAKING CUSTARDS: low comedy use of custard, similar to the pie-throwing of twentieth-century comedy.
23. ROUT: mob.
24. GULL: simpleton; OLD ENDS: familiar tags.
27. MAKE . . . FACTION: win the approval of the insane inmates of Bethlehem Hospital.
30. QUICK: lively.
34. COPPERAS: vitriol.

(I.i.)
5. RAM: the zodiacal sign of Aries.
10. THE CENTER: the earth's core.
15. THAT AGE: the classical Golden Age.
19. THEY . . . ASCRIBE: when Venus was called "golden."
25. TO BOOT: in addition.

ACT I

Scene I

[Enter Volpone and Mosca.]

Volp. Good morning to the day; and next, my gold!—
Open the shrine, that I may see my saint.
[Mosca draws a curtain and reveals a heap of gold.]
Hail the world's soul, and mine! More glad than is
The teeming earth to see the longed-for sun
Peep through the horns of the celestial Ram   5
Am I, to view thy splendor darkening his;
That lying here, amongst my other hoards,
Showst like a flame by night, or like the day
Struck out of chaos, when all darkness fled
Unto the center. O thou son of Sol,   10
But brighter than thy father, let me kiss,
With adoration, thee and every relic
Of sacred treasure in this blessed room.
Well did wise poets by thy glorious name
Title that age which they would have the best;   15
Thou being the best of things and far transcending
All style of joy in children, parents, friends,
Or any other waking dream on earth.
Thy looks when they to Venus did ascribe,
They should have giv'n her twenty thousand Cupids; 20
Such are thy beauties and our loves! Dear saint,
Riches, the dumb god, that givest all men tongues,
That canst do nought, and yet makest men do all
        things.
The price of souls! Even hell, with thee to boot,   25
Is made worth heaven. Thou art virtue, fame,

27

Honor, and all things else. Who can get thee,
He shall be noble, valiant, honest, wise—
   Mosca. And what he will, sir. Riches are in fortune
A greater good than wisdom is in nature.   30
   Volp. True, my beloved Mosca. Yet I glory
More in the cunning purchase of my wealth
Than in the glad possession, since I gain
No common way. I use no trade, no venture;
I wound no earth with plowshares, fat no beasts   35
To feed the shambles; have no mills for iron,
Oil, corn, or men, to grind 'em into powder;
I blow no subtle glass, expose no ships
To threat'nings of the furrow-faced sea;
I turn no moneys in the public bank,   40
Nor usure private—
   Mosca.   No, sir, nor devour
Soft prodigals. You shall ha' some will swallow
A melting heir as glibly as your Dutch
Will pills of butter and ne'er purge for 't;   45
Tear forth the fathers of poor families
Out of their beds, and coffin them alive
In some kind, clasping prison, where their bones
May be forthcoming when the flesh is rotten.
But your sweet nature doth abhor these courses;   50
You loathe the widow's or the orphan's tears
Should wash your pavements, or their piteous cries
Ring in your roofs and beat the air for vengeance.
   Volp. Right, Mosca, I do loathe it.
   Mosca.   And, besides, sir,   55
You are not like the thresher that doth stand

---

32. PURCHASE: acquisition.
34. VENTURE: gamble.
36. SHAMBLES: slaughterhouse.
41. USURE: engage in moneylending.
59. MALLOWS: wild plants.
61. ROMAGNIA: a sweet Greek wine; CANDIAN: Cretan.
66. OBSERVER: servant.
76. COCKER UP: indulge; GENIUS: appetite.
78. ALLY: kinsman.
80. OBSERVE: court.
81. CLIENTS: sycophants.
87. ENGROSS: monopolize.

With a huge flail, watching a heap of corn,
And, hungry, dares not taste the smallest grain,
But feeds on mallows and such bitter herbs;
Nor like the merchant who hath filled his vaults   60
With Romagnía and rich Candian wines,
Yet drinks the lees of Lombard's vinegar.
You will not lie in straw whilst moths and worms
Feed on your sumptuous hangings and soft beds.
You know the use of riches and dare give now   65
From that bright heap to me, your poor observer,
Or to your dwarf, or your hermaphrodite,
Your eunuch, or what other household trifle
Your pleasure allows maint'nance—

   Volp.   Hold thee, Mosca,   70
Take of my hand; thou strikest on truth in all,
And they are envious term thee parasite.
Call forth my dwarf, my eunuch, and my fool,
And let 'em make me sport!   [*Exit Mosca.*]
                What should I do   75
But cocker up my genius and live free
To all delights my fortune calls me to?
I have no wife, no parent, child, ally,
To give my substance to; but whom I make
Must be my heir, and this makes men observe me.   80
This draws new clients daily to my house,
Women and men of every sex and age,
That bring me presents, send me plate, coin, jewels,
With hope that when I die—which they expect
Each greedy minute—it shall then return   85
Tenfold upon them; whilst some, covetous
Above the rest, seek to engross me whole,
And counterwork the one unto the other,
Contend in gifts as they would seem in love.
All which I suffer, playing with their hopes,   90
And am content to coin 'em into profit,
And look upon their kindness, and take more,

And look on that; still bearing them in hand,
Letting the cherry knock against their lips,
And draw it by their mouths, and back again.   95
                                        How now!

[*Re-enter Mosca with Nano, Androgyno,
                and Castrone.*]

Nano. *Now, room for fresh gamesters, who do will
    you to know,*
They do bring you neither play nor university show;
And therefore do entreat you that whatsoever they re- 100
    hearse
*May not fare a whit the worse for the false pace of the
    verse.*
*If you wonder at this, you will wonder more ere we
    pass,*   105
For know, here is enclosed the soul of Pythagoras,
That juggler divine, as hereafter shall follow:
Which soul, fast and loose, sir, came first from Apollo,
And was breathed into Aethalides, Mercurius' son,
Where it had the gift to remember all that ever was   110
    done.
*From thence it fled forth and made quick transmigra-
    tion*

---

93. BEARING . . . HAND: deceiving them.
100-01: REHEARSE: recite.
108. FAST . . . LOOSE: a sleight-of-hand trick with a knot.
109. AETHALIDES: herald of the Argonauts.
114. EUPHORBUS: a Trojan hero.
116. CUCKOLD: Menelaus, cuckolded by Paris and Helen.
117. CHARTA: list.
121. SOPHIST: Pythagoras.
123. HIGHT: called; ASPASIA: famous mistress of Pericles; MERETRIX:
prostitute.
128. BROCK: badger.
129. COBBLER'S COCK: a dialogue of Lucian contains the story told
by a cobbler's cock that had been Pythagoras in one incarnation.
133. TRIGON: the number ten, symbolized by a triangle formed of ten
dots; GOLDEN THIGH: a legendary attribute of Pythagoras.
135. TRANSLATION: transformation.
141. CARTHUSIAN: a religious brotherhood with strict dietary regula-
tions. The Pythagorean sects abstained from fish.
142. SILENCE: a rule of five years' silence was imposed on the
Pythagoreans.
148. MOIL: mule.
150. BEANS: another Pythagorean prohibition.

*To goldy-locked Euphorbus, who was killed in good
      fashion*   115
At the siege of old Troy by the cuckold of Sparta.
Hermotimus was next—I find it in my charta—
To whom it did pass, where no sooner it was missing,
*But with one Pyrrhus of Delos it learned to go a-fish-
      ing;*   120
And thence did it enter the Sophist of Greece.
From Pythagore she went into a beautiful piece,
Hight Aspasia the Meretrix; and the next toss of her
Was again of a whore she became a philosopher,
Crates the Cynic, as itself doth relate it.   125
*Since, kings, knights, and beggars, knaves, lords, and
      fools gat it,*
Besides ox and ass, camel, mule, goat, and brock,
In all which it hath spoke, as in the cobbler's cock.
But I come not here to discourse of that matter,   130
*Or his one, two, or three, or his great oath, "By
      Quater!"*
His musics, his trigon, his golden thigh,
Or his telling how elements shift. But I
Would ask how of late thou hast suffered translation,   135
And shifted thy coat in these days of reformation?
      And. *Like one of the reformed, a fool, as you see,*
Counting all old doctrine heresy.
      Nano. *But not on thine own forbid meats hast thou
          ventured?*   140
      And. *On fish, when first a Carthusian I entered.*
      Nano. *Why, then thy dogmatical silence hath left
          thee?*
      And. *Of that an obstreperous lawyer bereft me.*
      Nano. *O wonderful change! When Sir Lawyer for-*   145
          sook thee,
For Pythagore's sake, what body then took thee?
      And. *A good dull moil.*
      Nano.   *And how! By that means*
Thou wert brought to allow of the eating of beans?   150

And. *Yes.*

Nano. *But from the moil into whom didst thou pass?*

And. *Into a very strange beast, by some writers
    called an ass;*

By others a precise, pure, illuminate brother,   155
Of those devour flesh and sometimes one another;
And will drop you forth a libel, or a sanctified lie,
Betwixt every spoonful of a nativity pie.

Nano. *Now quit thee, 'fore heaven, of that profane
    nation,*   160
And gently report thy next transmigration.

And. *To the same that I am.*

Nano.   *A creature of delight,*
And, what is more than a fool, an hermaphrodite!
Now, pray thee, sweet soul, in all thy variation,   165
*Which body wouldst thou choose to take up thy sta-
    tion?*

And. *Troth, this I am in; even here would I tarry.*

Nano. *'Cause here the delight of each sex thou canst
    vary?*   170

And. *Alas, those pleasures be stale and forsaken.*
No, 'tis your fool wherewith I am so taken,
The only one creature that I can call blessed;
For all other forms I have proved most distressed.

Nano. *Spoke true, as thou wert in Pythagoras still.*   175
This learned opinion we celebrate will,
*Fellow eunuch, as behooves us, with all our wit and
    art,*
*To dignify that whereof ourselves are so great and
    special a part.*   180

---

155. BROTHER: i.e., a Puritan.
158. NATIVITY PIE: the Puritan's name for a "Christmas pie."
160. NATION: kindred.
194. BAUBLE: baton surmounted by a fool's head, carried by the professional fool.
196. SLAUGHTER: punishment.
199. TRENCHER: wooden plate.
200. WIT: a wise man.
208. CHANGING: being changed.

Volp. Now, very, very pretty! Mosca, this
Was thy invention?
   Mosca.   If it please my patron,
Not else.
   Volp. It doth, good Mosca.   185
   Mosca.   Then it was, sir.

Song.

Fools they are the only nation
Worth men's envy or admiration;
Free from care or sorrow taking,
Selves and others merry making.   190
All they speak or do is sterling.
Your fool he is your great man's darling,
And your ladies' sport and pleasure;
Tongue and bauble are his treasure.
E'en his face begetteth laughter,   195
And he speaks truth free from slaughter.
He's the grace of every feast,
And sometimes the chiefest guest;
Hath his trencher and his stool,
When wit waits upon the fool.   200
   O, who would not be
     He, he, he?   *One knocks without.*

Volp. Who's that? Away! Look, Mosca.
             [Exeunt Nano and Castrone.]
   Mosca.   Fool, begone!
                [Exit Androgyno.]
'Tis Signor Voltore, the advocate.   205
I know him by his knock.
   Volp.   Fetch me my gown,
My furs and nightcaps; say my couch is changing;
And let him entertain himself awhile
Without i' the gallery.   *[Exit Mosca.]* 210
            Now, now my clients
Begin their visitation! Vulture, kite,

Raven, and gorcrow, all my birds of prey,
That think me turning carcass, now they come.
I am not for 'em yet.   215

[*Re-enter Mosca.*]

                    How now! The news?
  Mosca. A piece of plate, sir.
  Volp.   Of what bigness?
  Mosca.   Huge,
Massy, and antique, with your name inscribed   220
And arms engraven.
  Volp.   Good! And not a fox
Stretched on the earth, with fine delusive sleights,
Mocking a gaping crow? Ha, Mosca?
  Mosca.   Sharp, sir.   225
  Volp. Give me my furs. Why dost thou laugh so,
    man?
  Mosca. I cannot choose, sir, when I apprehend
What thoughts he has without now, as he walks:
That this might be the last gift he should give;   230
That this would fetch you; if you died today
And gave him all what he should be tomorrow;
What large return would come of all his ventures;
How he should worshiped be and reverenced;
Ride with his furs and footcloths, waited on   235
By herds of fools and clients; have clear way
Made for his moil, as lettered as himself;
Be called the great and learned advocate;
And then concludes there's nought impossible.
  Volp. Yes, to be learned, Mosca.   240
  Mosca.   O, no! rich
Implies it. Hood an ass with reverend purple,

---

213. GORCROW: carrion crow.
235. FOOTCLOTHS: horse's trappings.
237. LETTERED: learned.
243. AMBITIOUS: towering.
262. POSTURE: pose.
268. NOTES: signs.

So you can hide his two ambitious ears,
And he shall pass for a cathedral doctor.
    Volp. My caps, my caps, good Mosca. Fetch him in. 245
    Mosca. Stay, sir, your ointment for your eyes.
    Volp.   That's true;
Dispatch, dispatch. I long to have possession
Of my new present.
    Mosca.   That and thousands more 250
I hope to see you lord of.
    Volp.   Thanks, kind Mosca.
    Mosca. And that, when I am lost in blended dust,
And hundred such as I am, in succession—
    Volp. Nay, that were too much, Mosca. 255
    Mosca.   You shall live
Still to delude these harpies.
    Volp.   Loving Mosca!
'Tis well; my pillow now, and let him enter.
                      [Exit Mosca.]
Now my feigned cough, my phthisic, and my gout, 260
My apoplexy, palsy, and catarrhs,
Help, with your forced functions, this my posture,
Wherein this three year I have milked their hopes.
He comes; I hear him—Uh! *[Coughing]* uh! uh! uh! O!

      [Re-enter Mosca with Voltore.]

    Mosca. You still are what you were, sir. Only you, 265
Of all the rest, are he commands his love;
And you do wisely to preserve it thus
With early visitation and kind notes
Of your good meaning to him, which, I know,
Cannot but come most grateful. Patron! Sir! 270
Here's Signor Voltore is come—
    Volp. *[Faintly]*   What say you?
    Mosca. Sir, Signor Voltore is come this morning
To visit you.
    Volp.   I thank him. 275

Mosca.   And hath brought
A piece of antique plate, bought of St. Mark,
With which he here presents you.
    Volp.   He is welcome.
Pray him to come more often.   280
    Mosca.   Yes.
    Volt.   What says he?
    Mosca. He thanks you and desires you see him
    often.
    Volp. Mosca.   285
    Mosca.   My patron!
    Volp.   Bring him near; where is he?
I long to feel his hand.
    Mosca.   The plate is here, sir.
    Volt. How fare you, sir?   290
    Volp.   I thank you, Signor Voltore.
Where is the plate? Mine eyes are bad.
    Volt.   I'm sorry
To see you still thus weak.
    Mosca. [*Aside*]   That he is not weaker.   295
    Volp. You are too munificent.
    Volt.   No, sir, would to heaven
I could as well give health to you as that plate.
    Volp. You give, sir, what you can. I thank you. Your
    love   300
Hath taste in this and shall not be unanswered.
I pray you see me often.
    Volt.   Yes, I shall, sir.
    Volp. Be not far from me.
    Mosca.   Do you observe that, sir? 305
    Volp. Hearken unto me still; it will concern you.
    Mosca. You are a happy man, sir; know your good.
    Volp. I cannot now last long—
    Mosca.   You are his heir, sir.

---

277. OF ST. MARK: in the Piazza San Marco, where there were many
shops.
321. WRITE . . . FAMILY: employ me in your household.
343. COURSE: profession.

Volt. Am I?   310

Volp. I feel me going. Uh! uh! uh! uh!
I am sailing to my port. Uh! uh! uh! uh!
And I am glad I am so near my haven.
  Mosca. Alas, kind gentleman! Well, we must all go—
Volt. But, Mosca—   315
Mosca.   Age will conquer.
Volt.   Pray thee hear me.
Am I inscribed his heir for certain?
  Mosca.   Are you!
I do beseech you, sir, you will vouchsafe   320
To write me i' your family. All my hopes
Depend upon your Worship. I am lost
Except the rising sun do shine on me.
  Volt. It shall both shine and warm thee, Mosca.
  Mosca.   Sir,   325
I am a man that have not done your love
All the worst offices: here I wear your keys,
See all your coffers and your caskets locked,
Keep the poor inventory of your jewels,
Your plate and moneys; am your steward, sir;   330
Husband your goods here.
    Volt.   But am I sole heir?
  Mosca. Without a partner, sir, confirmed this morn-
          ing;
The wax is warm yet and the ink scarce dry   335
Upon the parchment.
    Volt.   Happy, happy me!
By what good chance, sweet Mosca?
  Mosca.   Your desert, sir;
I know no second cause.   340
    Volt.   Thy modesty
Is loath to know it; well, we shall requite it.
  Mosca. He ever liked your course, sir; that first took
          him.
I oft have heard him say how he admired   345

Men of your large profession, that could speak
To every cause, and things mere contraries,
Till they were hoarse again, yet all be law;
That, with most quick agility, could turn
And return, make knots and undo them,   350
Give forked counsel, take provoking gold
On either hand, and put it up. These men,
He knew, would thrive with their humility.
And, for his part, he thought he should be blest
To have his heir of such a suffering spirit,   355
So wise, so grave, of so perplexed a tongue
And loud withal, that would not wag nor scarce
Lie still without a fee; when every word
Your Worship but lets fall is a *cecchine.*

                                    Another knocks.

Who's that? One knocks; I would not have you seen, 360
    sir.
And yet—pretend you came and went in haste;
I'll fashion an excuse. And, gentle sir,
When you do come to swim in golden lard,
Up to the arms in honey, that your chin   365
Is borne up stiff with fatness of the flood,
Think on your vassal; but remember me.
I ha' not been your worst of clients.
    Volt.   Mosca—
    Mosca. When will you have your inventory brought, 370
    sir?
Or see a copy of the will?—Anon!—
I'll bring 'em to you, sir. Away, begone,
Put business i' your face.   [*Exit Voltore.*]

---

346. LARGE: wide-ranging.
347. MERE: downright.
351. FORKED: equivocal; PROVOKING: bribing.
352. PUT . . . UP: conceal it.
355. SUFFERING: tolerant.
356. PERPLEXED: complicated (producing confusion).
359. CECCHINE: *zecchino,* gold coin of Venice.
366. FATNESS: luxuriance.
368. CLIENTS: followers.
372. ANON: coming!
408. PHYSIC: medicine.

Volp. [*Springing up*] Excellent, Mosca!   375
Come hither, let me kiss thee.
   Mosca.   Keep you still, sir.
Here is Corbaccio.
   Volp.   Set the plate away.
The vulture's gone and the old raven's come.   380
   Mosca. Betake you to your silence and your sleep.
Stand there and multiply. [*Adds plate to his hoard.*]
    Now shall we see
A wretch who is indeed more impotent
Than this can feign to be, yet hopes to hop   385
Over his grave.

[*Enter Corbaccio.*]

    Signor Corbaccio!
You're very welcome, sir.
   Corb.   How does your patron?
   Mosca. Troth, as he did, sir; no amends.   390
   Corb.   What! Mends he?
   Mosca. No, sir, he is rather worse.
   Corb.   That's well. Where is he?
   Mosca. Upon his couch, sir, newly fall'n asleep.
   Corb. Does he sleep well?   395
   Mosca.   No wink, sir, all this night
Nor yesterday, but slumbers.
   Corb.   Good! He should take
Some counsel of physicians: I have brought him
An opiate here from mine own doctor.   400
   Mosca. He will not hear of drugs.
   Corb.   Why? I myself
Stood by while 'twas made, saw all the ingredients;
And know it cannot but most gently work.
My life for his, 'tis but to make him sleep.   405
   Volp. [*Aside*] Ay, his last sleep, if he would take it.
   Mosca.   Sir,
He has no faith in physic.

Corb.   Say you? Say you?

Mosca. He has no faith in physic; he does think   410
Most of your doctors are the greater danger
And worse disease t' escape. I often have
Heard him protest that your physician
Should never be his heir.

Corb.   Not I his heir?   415

Mosca. Not your physician, sir.

Corb.   O, no, no, no!
I do not mean it.

Mosca.   No, sir, nor their fees
He cannot brook; he says they flay a man   420
Before they kill him.

Corb.   Right, I do conceive you.

Mosca. And then, they do it by experiment;
For which the law not only doth absolve 'em
But gives them great reward; and he is loath   425
To hire his death so.

Corb.   It is true; they kill
With as much license as a judge.

Mosca.   Nay, more;
For he but kills, sir, where the law condemns,   430
And these can kill him too.

Corb.   Ay, or me,
Or any man. How does his apoplex?
Is that strong on him still?

Mosca.   Most violent.   435
His speech is broken and his eyes are set,
His face drawn longer than 'twas wont—

Corb.   How? How?
Stronger than he was wont?

411. YOUR DOCTORS: doctors as a class.
422. CONCEIVE: understand.
423. BY: by way of.
456. FORTH: out of; RESOLVED: reduced to a watery state.
459. SCOTOMY: dizziness.
460. LEFT: ceased.

Mosca.   No, sir; his face   440
Drawn longer than 'twas wont.
    Corb.   O, good!
    Mosca.   His mouth
Is ever gaping, and his eyelids hang.
    Corb.   Good.   445
    Mosca. A freezing numbness stiffens all his joints
And makes the color of his flesh like lead.
    Corb.   'Tis good.
    Mosca. His pulse beats slow and dull.
    Corb.   Good symptoms still!   450
    Mosca. And from his brain—
    Corb.   Ha? How? Not from his brain?
    Mosca. Yes, sir, and from his brain—
    Corb.   I conceive you; good!
    Mosca. Flows a cold sweat, with a continual rheum   455
Forth the resolved corners of his eyes.
    Corb. Is't possible? Yet I am better, ha!
How does he with the swimming of his head?
    Mosca. O, sir, 'tis past the scotomy; he now
Hath lost his feeling and hath left to snort;   460
You hardly can perceive him that he breathes.
    Corb. Excellent, excellent! Sure I shall outlast him!
This makes me young again a score of years.
    Mosca. I was a-coming for you, sir.
    Corb.   Has he made his will?   465
What has he giv'n me?
    Mosca.   No, sir.
    Corb.   Nothing? Ha?
    Mosca. He has not made his will, sir.
    Corb.   O, O, O!   470
What then did Voltore, the lawyer, here?
    Mosca. He smelt a carcass, sir, when he but heard
My master was about his testament;
As I did urge him to it, for your good—
    Corb. He came unto him, did he? I thought so.   475
    Mosca. Yes, and presented him this piece of plate.

Corb. To be his heir?

Mosca.   I do not know, sir.

Corb.   True,
I know it too.   480

Mosca. [*Aside*] By your own scale, sir.

Corb.   Well,
I shall prevent him yet. See, Mosca, look,
Here I have brought a bag of bright *cecchines*
Will quite weigh down his plate.   485

Mosca.   Yea, marry, sir,
This is true physic, this your sacred medicine!
No talk of opiates to this great elixir!

Corb. 'Tis *aurum palpabile*, if not *potabile*.

Mosca. It shall be ministered to him in his bowl.   490

Corb. Ay, do, do, do!

Mosca.   Most blessed cordial!
This will recover him.

Corb.   Yes, do, do, do!

Mosca. I think it were not best, sir.   495

Corb.   What?

Mosca.   To recover him.

Corb. O, no, no, no; by no means!

Mosca.   Why, sir, this
Will work some strange effect, if he but feel it.   500

Corb. 'Tis true, therefore forbear; I'll take my ven-
     ture;
Give me 't again.

Mosca.   At no hand, pardon me;
You shall not do yourself that wrong, sir. I   505
Will so advise you, you shall have it all.

---

483. PREVENT: forestall.
489. AURUM PALPABILE: tangible gold; POTABILE: drinkable (in
medicine: an alchemist's remedy).
501-02. VENTURE: investment (his gift).
504. AT . . . HAND: not at all.
528. COLOR: pretense.
529. TAKING: convincing.
532. ENFORCE: stress.
533. WATCHINGS: vigils.
536. PROPER ISSUE: own offspring.
537. BRAVE: noble.

Corb. How?

Mosca. All, sir; 'tis your right, your own; no man
Can claim a part. 'Tis yours without a rival,
Decreed by destiny.   510

    Corb.   How, how, good Mosca?

Mosca. I'll tell you, sir. This fit he shall recover—

Corb. I do conceive you.

Mosca.   And on first advantage
Of his gained sense will I re-importune him   515
Unto the making of his testament;
And show him this.   [*Points to the bag of coins.*]

    Corb.   Good, good.

Mosca.   'Tis better yet,
If you will hear, sir.   520

    Corb.   Yes, with all my heart.

Mosca. Now would I counsel you make home with
     speed;
There, frame a will, whereto you shall inscribe
My master your sole heir.   525

    Corb.   And disinherit
My son?

Mosca. O, sir, the better; for that color
Shall make it much more taking.

    Corb.   O, but color?   530

Mosca. This will, sir, you shall send it unto me.
Now, when I come to enforce, as I will do,
Your cares, your watchings, and your many prayers,
Your more than many gifts, your this day's present;
And last, produce your will, where, without thought 535
Or least regard unto your proper issue,
A son so brave and highly meriting,
The stream of your diverted love hath thrown you
Upon my master and made him your heir;
He cannot be so stupid or stone-dead   540
But out of conscience and mere gratitude—

    Corb. He must pronounce me his?

Mosca. 'Tis true.

Corb. This plot
Did I think on before. 545

Mosca. I do believe it.

Corb. Do you not believe it?

Mosca. Yes, sir.

Corb. Mine own project.

Mosca. Which, when he hath done, sir— 550

Corb. Published me his heir?

Mosca. And you so certain to survive him—

Corb. Ay.

Mosca. Being so lusty a man—

Corb. 'Tis true. 555

Mosca. Yes, sir—

Corb. I thought on that, too. See, how he should be
The very organ to express my thoughts!

Mosca. You have not only done yourself a good—

Corb. But multiplied it on my son! 560

Mosca. 'Tis right, sir.

Corb. Still my invention.

Mosca. 'Las, sir! Heaven knows,
It hath been all my study, all my care—
I e'en grow gray withal—how to work things— 565

Corb. I do conceive, sweet Mosca.

Mosca. You are he
For whom I labor here.

Corb. Ay, do, do, do!
I'll straight about it. 570

Mosca. [*Aside*] Rook go with you, raven!

Corb. I know thee honest.

Mosca. [*Aside*] You do lie, sir!

Corb. And—

---

562. STILL . . . INVENTION: i.e., Mosca's plan, as always, agrees with
his own.
570. STRAIGHT: at once.
571. ROOK: the appellation "rook" (simpleton; dupe).
578. GULL: cheat.
589. FLUX: discharge.
595. GIVE . . . WORDS: deceive them.
596. POUR . . . EARS: flatter them falsely.

Mosca. [*Aside*] Your knowledge is no better than 575
    your ears, sir.
Corb. I do not doubt to be a father to thee.
Mosca. [*Aside*] Nor I to gull my brother of his
    blessing.
Corb. I may ha' my youth restored to me; why not? 580
Mosca. [*Aside*] Your Worship is a precious ass!
Corb.   What sayst thou?
Mosca. I do desire your Worship to make haste, sir.
Corb. 'Tis done, 'tis done; I go.   [*Exit.*]
Volp. (*Leaping from his couch*) O, I shall 585
    burst!
Let out my sides, let out my sides—
    Mosca.   Contain
Your flux of laughter, sir. You know this hope
Is such a bait it covers any hook.   590
    Volp. O, but thy working and thy placing it!
I cannot hold; good rascal, let me kiss thee!
I never knew thee in so rare a humor.
    Mosca. Alas, sir, I but do as I am taught;
Follow your grave instructions; give 'em words;   595
Pour oil into their ears; and send them hence.
    Volp. 'Tis true, 'tis true. What a rare punishment
Is avarice to itself!
    Mosca.   Ay, with our help, sir.
    Volp. So many cares, so many maladies,   600
So many fears attending on old age,
Yea, death so often called on as no wish
Can be more frequent with 'em; their limbs faint,
Their senses dull, their seeing, hearing, going,
All dead before them; yea, their very teeth,   605
Their instruments of eating, failing them;
Yet this is reckoned life! Nay, here was one
Is now gone home that wishes to live longer!
Feels not his gout nor palsy; feigns himself
Younger by scores of years; flatters his age   610

With confident belying it; hopes he may
With charms, like Aeson, have his youth restored;
And with these thoughts so battens as if fate
Would be as easily cheated on as he,
And all turns air! (*Another knocks.*) Who's that there,   615
    now? A third?

   Mosca. Close, to your couch again. I hear his voice.
It is Corvino, our spruce merchant.

    Volp. [*Lies down as before*] Dead.

    Mosca. Another bout, sir, with your eyes.   620
                       [*Anoints them.*]

    Who's there?

[*Enter Corvino.*]

Signor Corvino! Come most wished for! O,
How happy were you, if you knew it, now!

   Corv. Why? What? Wherein?

   Mosca.   The tardy hour is come, sir.   625

   Corv. He is not dead?

   Mosca.   Not dead, sir, but as good;
He knows no man.

   Corv.   How shall I do, then?

   Mosca.   Why, sir?   630

   Corv. I have brought him here a pearl.

   Mosca.   Perhaps he has
So much remembrance left as to know you, sir;
He still calls on you; nothing but your name
Is in his mouth. Is your pearl orient, sir?   635

   Corv. Venice was never owner of the like.

   Volp. [*Faintly*] Signor Corvino.

   Mosca.   Hark.

   Volp.   Signor Corvino.

---

612. Aeson: father of Jason, rejuvenated by Medea's magic.
613. battens: stuffs himself.
617. close: be careful.
635. orient: Oriental, therefore of superior value.
658. visor: mask.

Mosca. He calls you; step and give it to him. He's 640
   here, sir,
And he has brought you a rich pearl.
   Corv.   How do you, sir?
Tell him it doubles the twelfth carat.
   Mosca.   Sir, 645
He cannot understand; his hearing's gone;
And yet it comforts him to see you—
   Corv.   Say
I have a diamond for him, too.
   Mosca.   Best show't, sir, 650
Put it into his hand; 'tis only there
He apprehends. He has his feeling yet.
See how he grasps it!
   Corv.   'Las, good gentleman!
How pitiful the sight is! 655
   Mosca.   Tut! forget, sir.
The weeping of an heir should still be laughter
Under a visor.
   Corv.   Why, am I his heir?
   Mosca. Sir, I am sworn; I may not show the will 660
Till he be dead; but here has been Corbaccio,
Here has been Voltore, here were others too,
I cannot number 'em, they were so many,
All gaping here for legacies; but I,
Taking the vantage of his naming you, 665
"Signor Corvino," "Signor Corvino," took
Paper and pen and ink, and there I asked him
Whom he would have his heir? "Corvino!" Who
Should be executor? "Corvino!" And
To any question he was silent to 670
I still interpreted the nods he made,
Through weakness, for consent; and sent home the
   others,
Nothing bequeathed them but to cry and curse.
   Corv. O my dear Mosca! (*They embrace.*) Does he 675
   not perceive us?

    Mosca. No more than a blind harper. He knows no
    man,
No face of friend nor name of any servant,
Who 'twas that fed him last or gave him drink;   680
Not those he hath begotten or brought up
Can he remember.
    Corv.   Has he children?
    Mosca.   Bastards,
Some dozen or more that he begot on beggars,   685
Gypsies, and Jews, and blackmoors, when he was
    drunk.
Knew you not that, sir? 'Tis the common fable.
The dwarf, the fool, the eunuch, are all his;
He's the true father of his family,   690
In all save me—but he has giv'n 'em nothing.
    Corv. That's well, that's well! Art sure he does not
    hear us?
    Mosca. Sure, sir? Why, look you, credit your own
    sense.   [*Shouts in Volpone's ear.*] 695
The pox approach and add to your diseases,
If it would send you hence the sooner, sir.
For your incontinence it hath deserved it
Throughly and throughly, and the plague to boot!—
You may come near, sir.—Would you would once close 700
Those filthy eyes of yours, that flow with slime
Like two frog pits; and those same hanging cheeks,
Covered with hide instead of skin—nay, help, sir—
That look like frozen dishclouts set on end.
    Corv. Or like an old smoked wall on which the rain 705
Ran down in streaks.
    Mosca.   Excellent, sir! Speak out;
You may be louder yet. A culverin
Discharged in his ear would hardly bore it.

---

696. pox: venereal disease.
699. THROUGHLY: thoroughly.
708. CULVERIN: cannon.
717. KEEP: care for.
737. GALLANT: handsome.
745. TURK: Sultan of Turkey.

Corv. His nose is like a common sewer, still running.   710
Mosca. 'Tis good! And what his mouth?
Corv.   A very draught.
Mosca. O, stop it up—
Corv.   By no means.
Mosca.   Pray you let me.   715
Faith, I could stifle him rarely with a pillow,
As well as any woman that should keep him.
Corv. Do as you will, but I'll be gone.
Mosca.   Be so;
It is your presence makes him last so long.   720
Corv. I pray you use no violence.
Mosca.   No, sir? Why?
Why should you be thus scrupulous, pray you, sir?
Corv. Nay, at your discretion.
Mosca.   Well, good sir, begone. 725
Corv. I will not trouble him now to take my pearl.
Mosca. Pooh! Nor your diamond. What a needless
    care
Is this afflicts you? Is not all here yours?
Am not I here, whom you have made your creature,   730
That owe my being to you?
Corv.   Grateful Mosca!
Thou art my friend, my fellow, my companion,
My partner, and shalt share in all my fortunes.
Mosca. Excepting one.   735
Corv.   What's that?
Mosca.   Your gallant wife, sir.
                              [*Exit Corvino.*]
Now is he gone. We had no other means
To shoot him hence but this.
Volp.   My divine Mosca!   740
Thou hast today outgone thyself.   *Another knocks.*
    Who's there?
I will be troubled with no more. Prepare
Me music, dances, banquets, all delights;
The Turk is not more sensual in his pleasures   745

Than will Volpone. Let me see, a pearl!

[*Exit Mosca.*]

A diamond! Plate! *Cecchines!* Good morning's pur-
    chase.

Why, this is better than rob churches yet!

Or fat, by eating once a month a man—   750

[*Re-enter Mosca.*]

Who is 't?

  Mosca. The beautous Lady Wouldbe, sir,

Wife to the English knight, Sir Politic Wouldbe—

This is the style, sir, is directed me—

Hath sent to know how you have slept tonight,   755

And if you would be visited?

  Volp.   Not now.

Some three hours hence—

  Mosca.   I told the squire so much.

  Volp. When I am high with mirth and wine, then, 760
    then.

'Fore heaven, I wonder at the desperate valor

Of the bold English, that they dare let loose

Their wives to all encounters!

  Mosca.   Sir, this knight   765

Had not his name for nothing; he is politic

And knows, howe'er his wife affect strange airs,

She hath not yet the face to be dishonest.

But had she Signor Corvino's wife's face—

  Volp. Has she so rare a face?   770

  Mosca.   O, sir, the wonder,

The blazing star of Italy! A wench

O' the first year! A beauty ripe as harvest!

Whose skin is whiter than a swan all over!

Than silver, snow, or lilies! A soft lip   775

---

759. SQUIRE: attendant.
768. FACE: (1) good looks; (2) courage; DISHONEST: unchaste.
793. CHARGE: duty.

Would tempt you to eternity of kissing!
And flesh that melteth in the touch to blood!
Bright as your gold, and lovely as your gold!
   Volp. Why had not I known this before?
   Mosca.   Alas, sir,   780
Myself but yesterday discovered it.
   Volp. How might I see her?
   Mosca.   O, not possible.
She's kept as warily as is your gold;
Never does come abroad, never takes air   785
But at a window. All her looks are sweet
As the first grapes or cherries and are watched
As near as they are.
   Volp.   I must see her!
   Mosca.   Sir,   790
There is a guard of ten spies thick upon her—
All his whole household—each of which is set
Upon his fellow and have all their charge,
When he goes out, when he comes in, examined.
   Volp. I will go see her, though but at her window. 795
   Mosca. In some disguise, then.
   Volp.   That is true. I must
Maintain mine own shape still the same. We'll think.
                        [Exeunt.]

ACT II

Scene I

[Enter Sir Politic Wouldbe and Peregrine.]

Sir Pol. Sir, to a wise man, all the world's his soil.
It is not Italy, nor France, nor Europe
That must bound me, if my fates call me forth.
Yet, I protest, it is no salt desire
Of seeing countries, shifting a religion,   5
Nor any disaffection to the state
Where I was bred and unto which I owe
My dearest plots hath brought me out; much less
That idle, antique, stale, gray-headed project
Of knowing men's minds and manners with Ulysses;   10
But a peculiar humor of my wife's,
Laid for this height of Venice, to observe,
To quote, to learn the language, and so forth—
I hope you travel, sir, with license?
    Per.   Yes.   15
    Sir Pol. I dare the safelier converse—How long, sir,
Since you left England?
    Per.   Seven weeks.
    Sir Pol.   So lately!
You ha' not been with my Lord Ambassador?   20

(II.i.)
4. SALT: immoderate.
12. HEIGHT: latitude.
13. QUOTE: make note of.
14. LICENSE: official permit (travel abroad was subject to government approval).
22. VENTS: issues from.
31. TROW: I wonder.
33. SPEAKS: denotes.
37. INTELLIGENCE: news.
38. TIRES: headdresses.
43. CRY . . . MERCY: beg your pardon.
50. PRODIGIES: portentous wonders; FIRES . . . BERWICK: an apparition of fighting men, accompanied by the sound of shooting, was reported from Berwick early in 1605.

Per. Not yet, sir.

Sir Pol.   Pray you, what news, sir, vents our
     climate?
I heard last night a most strange thing reported
By some of my lord's followers, and I long   25
To hear how 'twill be seconded!

Per.   What was't, sir?

Sir Pol. Marry, sir, of a raven that should build
In a ship royal of the King's.

Per. [*Aside*]   This fellow,   30
Does he gull me, trow, or is gulled?—Your name, sir?

Sir Pol. My name is Politic Wouldbe.

Per. [*Aside*]   O, that speaks him.—
A knight, sir?

Sir Pol. A poor knight, sir.   35

Per.   Your lady
Lies here in Venice for intelligence
Of tires and fashions and behavior
Among the courtesans? The fine Lady Wouldbe?

Sir Pol. Yes, sir, the spider and the bee ofttimes   40
Suck from one flower.

Per.   Good Sir Politic,
I cry you mercy. I have heard much of you.
'Tis true, sir, of your raven.

Sir Pol.   On your knowledge?   45

Per. Yes, and your lion's whelping in the Tower.

Sir Pol. Another whelp?

Per.   Another, sir.

Sir Pol.   Now, heaven!
What prodigies be these? The fires at Berwick!   50
And the new star! These things concurring, strange!
And full of omen! Saw you those meteors?

Per. I did, sir.

Sir Pol.   Fearful! Pray you, sir, confirm me,
Were there three porpoises seen above the bridge,   55
As they give out?

Per.   Six, and a sturgeon, sir.

Sir Pol. I am astonished!

Per.   Nay, sir, be not so;
I'll tell you a greater prodigy than these—

Sir Pol. What should these things portend?

Per.   The very day—
Let me be sure—that I put forth from London,
There was a whale discovered in the river,
As high as Woolwich, that had waited there,
Few know how many months, for the subversion
Of the Stode fleet.

Sir Pol.   Is't possible? Believe it,
'Twas either sent from Spain or the Archdukes!
Spinola's whale, upon my life, my credit!
Will they not leave these projects? Worthy sir,
Some other news.

Per.   Faith, Stone the fool is dead,
And they do lack a tavern fool extremely.

Sir Pol. Is Mas' Stone dead?

Per.   He's dead, sir; why, I hope
You thought him not immortal? [*Aside*] O, this knight,
Were he well known, would be a precious thing
To fit our English stage. He that should write
But such a fellow should be thought to feign
Extremely, if not maliciously.

Sir Pol.   Stone dead!

Per. Dead. Lord, how deeply, sir, you apprehend it!
He was no kinsman to you?

---

65. HIGH: far up the river.
67. STODE: Stade near Hamburg.
69. THE ARCHDUKES: Albert of Austria and his wife, the Infanta Isabella, who ruled the Spanish Netherlands from 1596.
70. SPINOLA: Ambrogio Spinola, commander of the Spanish army in the Netherlands from 1604. His legendary ingenuity inspired the rumor of a whale designed to flood London by spouting forth the Thames.
75. MAS': abbreviation of "Master."
83. APPREHEND: feel.
102. ORDINARY: tavern.
103. ADVERTISEMENT: information.
110. CHARACTER: cipher.
115. POLITY: craft.
117. TO 'T: in addition; NODDLE: brain.
121. MAMALUCHI: Mamelukes (slaves in Egypt during the Turkish domination).

   Sir Pol.   That I know of.   85
Well, that same fellow was an unknown fool.
   Per. And yet you knew him, it seems?
   Sir Pol.   I did so. Sir,
I knew him one of the most dangerous heads
Living within the state, and so I held him.   90
   Per. Indeed, sir?
   Sir Pol.   While he lived, in action.
He has received weekly intelligence,
Upon my knowledge, out of the Low Countries,
For all parts of the world, in cabbages;   95
And those dispensed again t'ambassadors,
In oranges, muskmelons, apricots,
Lemons, pomecitrons, and suchlike; sometimes
In Colchester oysters and your Selsey cockles.
   Per. You make me wonder!   100
   Sir Pol.   Sir, upon my knowledge.
Nay, I have observed him, at your public ordinary,
Take his advertisement from a traveler—
A concealed statesman—in a trencher of meat;
And instantly, before the meal was done,   105
Convey an answer in a toothpick.
   Per.   Strange!
How could this be, sir?
   Sir Pol.   Why, the meat was cut
So like his character, and so laid, as he   110
Must easily read the cipher.
   Per.   I have heard
He could not read, sir.
   Sir Pol.   So 'twas given out,
In polity, by those that did employ him.   115
But he could read and had your languages,
And to 't as sound a noddle—
   Per.   I have heard, sir,
That your baboons were spies, and that they were
A kind of subtle nation near to China.   120
   Sir Pol. Ay, ay, your *Mamaluchi*. Faith, they had

Their hand in a French plot or two; but they
Were so extremely given to women as
They made discovery of all. Yet I
Had my advices here, on Wednesday last,   125
From one of their own coat, they were returned,
Made their relations, as the fashion is,
And now stand fair for fresh employment.
    Per. [*Aside*]   Heart!
This Sir Poll will be ignorant of nothing.—   130
It seems, sir, you know all.
    Sir Pol.   Not all, sir, but
I have some general notions. I do love
To note and to observe. Though I live out,
Free from the active torrent, yet I'ld mark   135
The currents and the passages of things
For mine own private use; and know the ebbs
And flows of state.
    Per.   Believe it, sir, I hold
Myself in no small tie unto my fortunes   140
For casting me thus luckily upon you,
Whose knowledge, if your bounty equal it,
May do me great assistance in instruction
For my behavior and my bearing, which
Is yet so rude and raw—   145
    Sir Pol.   Why? Came you forth
Empty of rules for travel?
    Per.   Faith, I had
Some common ones, from out that vulgar grammar,
Which he that cried Italian to me taught me.   150

----

127. RELATIONS: reports.
140. IN: under; TIE: obligation.
150. CRIED: enunciated in teaching.
151-52. BRAVE BLOODS: fine gallants.
155. INGENUOUS: noble.
156. PROFESS: make a profession of.
163. BANK: bench.
165. DEAR: difficult.
171. VENTING: selling.
180. LEWD: base.
181. TERMS . . . SHREDS: medical phrases and old sayings.

Sir Pol. Why, this it is that spoils all our brave
    bloods:
Trusting our hopeful gentry unto pedants,
Fellows of outside and mere bark. You seem
To be a gentleman of ingenuous race—   155
I not profess it, but my fate hath been
To be where I have been consulted with,
In this high kind, touching some great men's sons,
Persons of blood and honor—

    [*Enter Mosca and Nano disguised, followed
               by Grege.*]

Per.   Who be these, sir?   160
Mosca. Under that window, there 't must be. The
    same.
Sir Pol. Fellows to mount a bank! Did your instruc-
    tor
In the dear tongues never discourse to you   165
Of the Italian mountebanks?
    Per.   Yes, sir.
    Sir Pol.   Why,
Here shall you see one.
    Per.   They are quacksalvers,   170
Fellows that live by venting oils and drugs.
    Sir Pol. Was that the character he gave you of them?
    Per. As I remember.
    Sir Pol.   Pity his ignorance.
They are the only knowing men of Europe!   175
Great general scholars, excellent physicians,
Most admired statesmen, professed favorites
And cabinet counselors to the greatest princes!
The only languaged men of all the world!
    Per. And I have heard they are most lewd impostors,   180
Made all of terms and shreds; no less beliers
Of great men's favors than their own vile med'cines;
Which they will utter, upon monstrous oaths,

Selling that drug for twopence, ere they part,
Which they have valued at twelve crowns before.   185
 Sir Pol. Sir, calumnies are answered best with silence.
Yourself shall judge. Who is it mounts, my friends?
 Mosca. Scoto of Mantua, sir.
 Sir Pol.   Is't he? Nay, then,
I'll proudly promise, sir, you shall behold   190
Another man than has been fant'sied to you.
I wonder yet that he should mount his bank
Here in this nook, that has been wont t' appear
In face of the Piazza. Here he comes.

 [*Enter Volpone disguised as a mountebank.*]

 Volp. [*To Nano*] Mount, zany.   195
 Grege. Follow, follow, follow, follow, follow.
 Sir Pol. See how the people follow him! He's a man
May write ten thousand crowns in bank here. Note,
Mark but his gesture. I do use to observe
The state he keeps in getting up.   200
 Per.   'Tis worth it, sir.
 Volp. Most noble gentlemen, and my worthy pa-
trons: It may seem strange that I, your Scoto Man-
tuano, who was ever wont to fix my bank in face of the
public Piazza, near the shelter of the portico to the   205
Procuratia, should now, after eight months' absence

---

188. Scoto: contemporary actor and sleight-of-hand artist.
191. FANT'SIED: portrayed.
194. PIAZZA: Piazza San Marco.
195. ZANY: stooge.
199. GESTURE: bearing.
200. STATE: dignity.
206. PROCURATIA: residence of the Procurators of St. Mark.
212. COLD . . . FEET: poverty-stricken.
217. SFORZATO: "constrained one," prisoner.
218. COOK: the dash indicates that the term is a euphemism; AT-
TACHED: impeached.
221. GROUND CIARLATANI: charlatans who make speeches from
ground level instead of from a platform.
222. FEATS . . . ACTIVITY: acrobatics.
224. TABARINE: Italian comic of the late sixteenth century; FABU-
LIST: storyteller.
234. SCARTOCCIOS: paper wrappers.
237-38. OPPILATIONS: obstructions.
240. HAP'ORTH: halfpenny-worth.

from this illustrious city of Venice, humbly retire myself into an obscure nook of the Piazza.

   Sir Pol. Did not I now object the same?

   Per.   Peace, sir.   210

   Volp. Let me tell you: I am not—as your Lombard
proverb saith—cold on my feet, or content to part with
my commodities at a cheaper rate than I accustomed;
look not for it. Nor that the calumnious reports of that
impudent detractor and shame to our profession— 215
Alessandro Buttone, I mean—who gave out in public
I was condemned a *sforzato* to the galleys for poison-
ing the Cardinal Bembo's—cook, hath at all attached,
much less dejected me. No, no, worthy gentlemen;
to tell you true, I cannot endure to see the rabble of 220
these ground *ciarlatani,* that spread their cloaks on
the pavement as if they meant to do feats of activity,
and then come in lamely with their moldy tales out of
Boccaccio like stale Tabarine, the fabulist; some of
them discoursing their travels and of their tedious 225
captivity in the Turk's galleys, when indeed, were the
truth known, they were the Christians' galleys, where
very temperately they eat bread and drunk water as a
wholesome penance enjoined them by their confessors
for base pilferies.   230

   Sir Pol. Note but his bearing and contempt of these.

   Volp. These turdy-facy-nasty-paty-lousy-fartical
rogues, with one poor groatsworth of unprepared an-
timony, finely wrapped up in several *scartoccios,* are
able very well to kill their twenty a week, and play. 235
Yet these meager, starved spirits, who have half
stopped the organs of their minds with earthly oppilations, want not their favorers among your shriveled,
salad-eating artisans, who are overjoyed that they may
have their hap'orth of physic; though it purge 'em in- 240
to another world, 't makes no matter.

   Sir Pol. Excellent! Ha' you heard better language,
    sir?

Volp. Well, let 'em go. And, gentlemen, honorable
gentlemen, know that for this time our bank, being 245
thus removed from the clamors of the *canáglia*, shall
be the scene of pleasure and delight; for I have nothing to sell, little or nothing to sell.

Sir Pol. I told you, sir, his end.

Per.   You did so, sir.   250

Volp. I protest, I and my six servants are not able
to make of this precious liquor so fast as it is fetched
away from my lodging by gentlemen of your city,
strangers of the Terra Firma, worshipful merchants,
ay, and senators too, who ever since my arrival have 255
detained me to their uses, by their splendidous liber-
alities. And worthily; for what avails your rich man to
have his magazines stuffed with *moscadelli,* or of the
purest grape, when his physicians prescribe him, on
pain of death, to drink nothing but water cocted with 260
aniseeds? O health! Health! The blessing of the rich!
The riches of the poor! Who can buy thee at too dear
a rate, since there is no enjoying this world without
thee? Be not then so sparing of your purses, honorable
gentlemen, as to abridge the natural course of life— 265

Per. You see his end?

Sir Pol.   Ay, is't not good?

Volp. For when a humid flux or catarrh, by the
mutability of air, falls from your head into an arm or

---

246. CANÁGLIA: rabble.
254. TERRA FIRMA: Italian mainland territory owned by Venice;
WORSHIPFUL: distinguished.
258. MAGAZINES: warehouses; MOSCADELLI: muscatel wines.
260. COCTED: boiled.
274. HUMORS: fluid secretions.
278. CRUDE: lacking power to digest.
281. UNCTION: salve; FRICACE: massage.
281-82. VERTIGINE: vertigo.
284. MAL CADUCO: falling sickness.
285. TREMOR CORDIA: palpitations of the heart.
285-86. RETIRED NERVES: shrunken sinews.
287. STRANGURY: urinary obstruction; HERNIA VENTOSA: abdominal
hernia; ILIACA PASSIO: colic.
288. TORSION: cramping.
296. ZAN FRITADA: a noted zany of the time.
299. STRANGELY: extraordinarily well.
301. BUT: except for.
302. BROUGHTON: Hugh Broughton, a Puritan preacher, whose works
concerned scriptural and rabbinical subjects.

shoulder or any other part; take you a ducat, or your 270
cecchine of gold, and apply to the place affected; see
what good effect it can work. No, no, 'tis this blessed
unguento, this rare extraction, that hath only power to
disperse all malignant humors that proceed either of
hot, cold, moist, or windy causes—   275

   Per. I would he had put in dry, too.

   Sir Pol.   Pray you observe.

   Volp. To fortify the most indigest and crude stom-
ach, ay, were it of one that, through extreme weakness, vomited blood, applying only a warm napkin to 280
the place, after the unction and fricace; for the *vertigine* in the head, putting but a drop into your nostrils, likewise behind the ears, a most sovereign and
approved remedy; the *mal caduco*, cramps, convul-
sions, paralyses, epilepsies, *tremor cordia*, retired 285
nerves, ill vapors of the spleen, stoppings of the liver,
the stone, the strangury, *hernia ventosa, iliaca passio;*
stops a *dysenteria* immediately; easeth the torsion of
the small guts; and cures *melancholia hypochondria-
ca*, being taken and applied according to my printed 290
receipt. (*Pointing to his bill and his glass.*) For this is
the physician, this the medicine; this counsels, this
cures; this gives the direction, this works the effect;
and, in sum, both together may be termed an abstract
of the theoric and practic in the Aesculapian art. 295
'Twill cost you eight crowns. And, Zan Fritada, pray
thee sing a verse extempore in honor of it.

   Sir Pol. How do you like him, sir?

   Per.   Most strangely, I!

   Sir Pol. Is not his language rare?   300

   Per.   But alchemy,
I never heard the like—or Broughton's books.

Song.

Had old Hippocrates or Galen,

That to their books put med'cines all in,
But known this secret, they had never—   305
Of which they will be guilty ever—
Been murderers of so much paper,
Or wasted many a hurtless taper.
No Indian drug had e'er been famed,
Tobacco, sassafras not named;   310
Ne yet of guacum one small stick, sir,
Nor Raymund Lully's great elixir.
Ne had been known the Danish Gonswart,
Or Paracelsus, with his longsword.

Per. All this yet will not do; eight crowns is high. 315
Volp. No more. Gentlemen, if I had but time to discourse to you the miraculous effects of this my oil, sur-
named *oglio del Scoto;* with the countless catalogue of
those I have cured of the aforesaid and many more
diseases; the patents and privileges of all the princes 320
and commonwealths of Christendom; or but the depo-
sitions of those that appeared on my part before the
signory of the *Sanità* and most learned college of
physicians; where I was authorized, upon notice taken
of the admirable virtues of my medicaments and mine 325
own excellency in matter of rare and unknown secrets
not only to disperse them publicly in this famous city
but in all the territories that happily joy under the
government of the most pious and magnificent states
of Italy. But may some other gallant fellow say, "O, 330
there be divers that make profession to have as good
and as experimented receipts as yours." Indeed, very

311. Ne: nor; GUACUM: guaiacum, a tropical tree bearing medicinal bark.
312. LULLY: Ramón Lull, medieval alchemist.
313. GONSWART: identity uncertain.
314. PARACELSUS: German physician and alchemist, who reputedly kept secret remedies in a hollow sword-pommel.
323. SIGNORY . . . SANITÀ: equivalent to commissioners of health.
331. DIVERS: various others.
337. SEVERAL SIMPLES: different herbs.
341. FUMO: smoke.
346. BOOK: record.
354. BALLOO: balloon ball, a popular sport.

many have assayed, like apes, in imitation of that
which is really and essentially in me, to make of this
oil; bestowed great cost in furnaces, stills, alembics, 335
continual fires, and preparation of the ingredients,—as
indeed there goes to it six hundred several simples,
besides some quantity of human fat, for the conglu-
tination, which we buy of the anatomists—but when
these practitioners come to the last decoction: blow, 340
blow, puff, puff, and all flies in *fumo*. Ha, ha, ha! Poor
wretches! I rather pity their folly and indiscretion
than their loss of time and money; for those may be
recovered by industry, but to be a fool born is a
disease incurable. For myself, I always from my youth 345
have endeavored to get the rarest secrets and book
them, either in exchange or for money. I spared nor
cost nor labor where anything was worthy to be
learned. And gentlemen, honorable gentlemen, I will
undertake, by virtue of chemical art, out of the honor- 350
able hat that covers your head to extract the four
elements: that is to say, the fire, air, water, and earth,
and return you your felt without burn or stain. For
whilst others have been at the balloo, I have been at
my book, and am now past the craggy paths of study 355
and come to the flowery plains of honor and reputation.

Sir Pol. I do assure you, sir, that is his aim.

Volp. But to our price—

Per. And that withal, Sir Poll. 360

Volp. You all know, honorable gentlemen, I never
valued this *ampulla*, or vial, at less than eight crowns;
but for this time I am content to be deprived of it for
six. Six crowns is the price, and less, in courtesy, I
know you cannot offer me. Take it or leave it, howso- 365
ever, both it and I am at your service. I ask you not as
the value of the thing, for then I should demand of
you a thousand crowns; so the Cardinals Montalto,

Farnese, the Great Duke of Tuscany, my gossip, with
divers other princes, have given me, but I despise 370
money. Only to show my affection to you, honorable
gentlemen, and your illustrious state here, I have neg-
lected the messages of these princes, mine own offices;
framed my journey hither only to present you with the
fruits of my travels. Tune your voices once more to 375
the touch of your instruments, and give the honorable
assembly some delightful recreation.

Per. What monstrous and most painful circumstance
Is here to get some three or four *gazets*,
Some threepence i' the whole! For that 'twill come to. 380

Song.

> You that would last long, list to my song;
> Make no more coil, but buy of this oil.
> Would you be ever fair and young?
> Stout of teeth and strong of tongue?
> Tart of palate? Quick of ear? 385
> Sharp of sight? Of nostril clear?
> Moist of hand and light of foot?
> Or I will come nearer to't—
> Would you live free from all diseases?
> Do the act your mistress pleases, 390
> Yet fright all aches from your bones?
> Here's a med'cine for the nones.

Volp. Well, I am in a humor at this time to make a
present of the small quantity my coffer contains; to the

369. GOSSIP: patron.
373. OFFICES: duties.
378. CIRCUMSTANCE: circumlocution.
379. GAZETS: Venetian coins.
382. COIL: ado.
392. NONES: nonce; specific purpose.
399-400. MUCCINIGO: another coin.
402. BATE: abate the price; BAGATINE: Venetian coin.
406. ADVERTISED: informed.
409-10. DOUBLE PISTOLET: Spanish gold coin.
411. SPARK: gallant.
414. GRACE: honor.

rich, in courtesy, and to the poor, for God's sake. 395
Wherefore now, mark: I asked you six crowns, and six
crowns, at other times, you have paid me. You shall
not give me six crowns, nor five, nor four, nor three,
nor two, nor one; nor half a ducat; no, nor a *muccinigo.* Six—pence it will cost you, or six hundred 400
pound—expect no lower price, for by the banner of
my front, I will not bate a *bagatine;* that I will have,
only, a pledge of your loves, to carry something from
amongst you to show I am not contemned by you.
Therefore now, toss your handkerchiefs, cheerfully, 405
cheerfully; and be advertised that the first heroic spirit
that deigns to grace me with a handkerchief, I will
give it a little remembrance of something beside shall
please it better than if I had presented it with a double pistolet.   410

Per. Will you be that heroic spark, Sir Poll?
Celia, at the window, throws down her handkerchief.
O, see, the window has prevented you!

Volp. Lady, I kiss your bounty; and for this timely
grace you have done your poor Scoto of Mantua I will
return you, over and above my oil, a secret of that 415
high and inestimable nature shall make you forever
enamored on that minute wherein your eye first
descended on so mean, yet not altogether to be
despised, an object. Here is a powder concealed in
this paper, of which, if I should speak to the worth, 420
nine thousand volumes were but as one page, that
page as a line, that line as a word; so short is this
pilgrimage of man, which some call life, to the ex-
pressing of it. Would I reflect on the price? Why, the
whole world were but as an empire, that empire as a 425
province, that province as a bank, that bank as a private purse, to the purchase of it. I will only tell you: it
is the powder that made Venus a goddess—given her
by Apollo—that kept her perpetually young, cleared
her wrinkles, firmed her gums, filled her skin, colored 430

her hair; from her derived to Helen, and at the sack
of Troy unfortunately lost; till now, in this our age, it
was as happily recovered by a studious antiquary out
of some ruins of Asia; who sent a moiety of it to the
court of France—but much sophisticated—wherewith   435
the ladies there now color their hair. The rest, at this
present, remains with me; extracted to a quintessence,
so that, wherever it but touches, in youth it perpetually preserves, in age restores the complexion; seats
your teeth, did they dance like virginal jacks, firm as a   440
wall; makes them white as ivory that were black as—

[*Enter Corvino.*]

   Corv. Spite o' the Devil, and my shame! Come
       down, here,
Come down! No house but mine to make your scene?
Signor Flaminio, will you down, sir? Down?   445
What, is my wife your *Franciscina*, sir?
No windows on the whole Piazza here,
To make your properties, but mine? But mine?
   He beats away [*Volpone, Mosca, Nano, and Grege*].
Heart! Ere tomorrow I shall be new christened,
And called the *Pantalone di Bisognosi*   450
About the town.
   Per. What should this mean, Sir Poll?
   Sir Pol. Some trick of state, believe it. I will home.
   Per. It may be some design on you.

---

431. DERIVED: given.
434. MOIETY: portion.
435. SOPHISTICATED: adulterated.
440. VIRGINAL JACKS: keys of a virginal.
445. SIGNOR FLAMINIO: Venetian actor.
446. FRANCISCINA: a servant-girl, one of the stock characters of
the *commedia dell' arte*.
450. PANTALONE DI BISOGNOSI: the usually cuckolded husband of
the *commedia dell' arte*, here with a last name indicating his descent
from paupers.

(II.ii.)
5. BOLTING: shooting darts.
8. AMBITIOUS: shooting high.
11. LIVER: reputed source of passion.

   Sir Pol.   I know not.   455
I'll stand upon my guard.
   Per.   It is your best, sir.
   Sir Pol. This three weeks, all my advices, all my let-
    ters,
They have been intercepted.   460
   Per.   Indeed, sir?
Best have a care.
   Sir Pol.   Nay, so I will.
   Per.   This knight,
I may not lose him, for my mirth, till night.   465
                     [Exeunt.]

Scene [II]

[Enter Volpone and Mosca.]

   Volp. O, I am wounded!
   Mosca.   Where, sir?
   Volp.   Not without;
Those blows were nothing. I could bear them ever.
But angry Cupid, bolting from her eyes,   5
Hath shot himself into me like a flame;
Where now he flings about his burning heat,
As in a furnace an ambitious fire
Whose vent is stopped. The fight is all within me.
I cannot live except thou help me, Mosca.   10
My liver melts, and I, without the hope
Of some soft air from her refreshing breath,
Am but a heap of cinders.
   Mosca.   'Las, good sir,
Would you had never seen her!   15
   Volp.   Nay, would thou
Hadst never told me of her!
   Mosca.   Sir, 'tis true;
I do confess I was unfortunate

And you unhappy; but I'm bound in conscience,   20
No less than duty, to effect my best
To your release of torment, and I will, sir.

    Volp. Dear Mosca, shall I hope?

    Mosca.   Sir, more than dear,
I will not bid you to despair of aught   25
Within a human compass.

    Volp.   O, there spoke
My better angel. Mosca, take my keys,
 Gold, plate, and jewels—all's at thy devotion.
Employ them how thou wilt; nay, coin me, too—   30
So thou in this but crown my longings, Mosca.

    Mosca. Use but your patience.

    Volp.   So I have.

    Mosca.   I doubt not
To bring success to your desires.   35

    Volp.   Nay, then,
I not repent me of my late disguise.

    Mosca. If you can horn him, sir, you need not.

    Volp.   True.
Besides, I never meant him for my heir.   40
Is not the color o' my beard and eyebrows
To make me known?

    Mosca.   No jot.

    Volp.   I did it well.

    Mosca. So well, would I could follow you in mine   45

---

26. COMPASS: range of achievement.
29. DEVOTION: service.
38. HORN: cuckold.
47. EPILOGUE: the beating from Corvino.

(II.iii.)

4. DOLE . . . FACES: changes of expression; grimaces.
12. TOADSTONE: stones mistakenly believed to come from the heads of toads were believed to have magic power.
13. COPE STITCH: embroidery stitch such as used on church vestments.
17. MOTHER: hysteria.
18. MOUNT: mount the stage with other mountebanks.
21. CITTERN: stringed instrument; VANITY: a morality play character.
22. DEALER: prostitute.

With half the happiness! And yet I would
Escape your epilogue.
   Volp.   But were they gulled
With a belief that I was Scoto?
   Mosca.   Sir,   50
Scoto himself could hardly have distinguished!
I have not time to flatter you now, we'll part;
And as I prosper, so applaud my art.
                                    [Exeunt.]

Scene [III]

[Enter Corvino, dragging in Celia.]

   Corv. Death of mine honor with the city's fool!
A juggling, tooth-drawing, prating mountebank!
And at a public window! Where, whilst he,
With his strained action and his dole of faces,
To his drug-lecture draws your itching ears,   5
A crew of old, unmarried, noted lechers
Stood leering up like satyrs; and you smile
Most graciously and fan your favors forth,
To give your hot spectators satisfaction!
What, was your mountebank their call? Their whistle?   10
Or were you enamored on his copper rings?
His saffron jewel with the toadstone in't?
Or his embroidered suit, with the cope stitch,
Made of a hearsecloth? Or his old tilt feather?
Or his starched beard? Well, you shall have him, yes!   15
He shall come home and minister unto you
The fricace for the mother. Or, let me see,
I think you'd rather mount; would you not mount?
Why, if you'll mount, you may; yes, truly, you may!
And so you may be seen, down to the foot.   20
Get you a cittern, Lady Vanity,
And be a dealer with the virtuous man;

Make one. I'll but protest myself a cuckold
And save your dowry. I am a Dutchman, I!
For if you thought me an Italian   25
You would be damned ere you did this, you whore!
Thou'dst tremble to imagine that the murder
Of father, mother, brother, all thy race,
Should follow, as the subject of my justice!
   Celia. Good sir, have patience.   30
   Corv.   What couldst thou propose
Less to thyself than, in this heat of wrath
And stung with my dishonor, I should strike
This steel into thee, with as many stabs
As thou wert gazed upon with goatish eyes?   35
   Celia. Alas, sir, be appeased! I could not think
My being at the window should more now
Move your impatience than at other times.
   Corv. No? Not to seek and entertain a parley
With a known knave before a multitude?   40
You were an actor with your handkerchief,
Which he most sweetly kissed in the receipt,
And might, no doubt, return it with a letter
And 'point the place where you might meet—your
   sister's,   45
Your mother's, or your aunt's might serve the turn.
   Celia. Why, dear sir, when do I make these excuses,
Or ever stir abroad but to the church?
And that so seldom—
   Corv.   Well, it shall be less;   50
And thy restraint before was liberty
To what I now decree. And therefore mark me:
First, I will have this bawdy light dammed up;
And till't be done, some two or three yards off
I'll chalk a line, o'er which if thou but chance   55
To set thy desp'rate foot, more hell, more horror,

---

  35. GOATISH: lecherous.
  70. PASSENGERS: passers-by.
  75. ANATOMY: cadaver.

More wild remorseless rage shall seize on thee
Than on a conjurer that had heedless left
His circle's safety ere his devil was laid.
Then, here's a lock which I will hang upon thee;   60
And, now I think on't, I will keep thee backwards;
Thy lodging shall be backwards, thy walks backwards,
Thy prospect—all be backwards, and no pleasure
That thou shalt know but backwards. Nay, since you force   65
My honest nature, know it is your own
Being too open makes me use you thus;
Since you will not contain your subtle nostrils
In a sweet room, but they must snuff the air
Of rank and sweaty passengers.   *Knock within.*   70
       One knocks.
Away, and be not seen, pain of thy life;
Not look toward the window; if thou dost—
Nay, stay, hear this—let me not prosper, whore,
But I will make thee an anatomy,   75
Dissect thee mine own self, and read a lecture
Upon thee to the city and in public.
Away!   [*Exit Celia.*]

                [*Enter Servitore.*]

    Who's there?
  Serv.   'Tis Signor Mosca, sir.   80
  Corv. Let him come in.   [*Exit Servitore.*]
       His master's dead! there's yet
Some good to help the bad.

                [*Enter Mosca.*]

                  My Mosca, welcome!
I guess your news.   85
  Mosca.   I fear you cannot, sir.
  Corv. Is't not his death?

Mosca.   Rather the contrary.

Corv. Not his recovery?

Mosca.   Yes, sir.   90

Corv.   I am cursed;
I am bewitched; my crosses meet to vex me.
How? How? How? How?

Mosca.   Why, sir, with Scoto's oil!
Corbaccio and Voltore brought of it   95
Whilst I was busy in an inner room—

   Corv. Death! That damned mountebank! But for
          the law
Now, I could kill the rascal; 't cannot be
His oil should have that virtue. Ha' not I   100
Known him, a common rogue, come fiddling in
To the *osteria* with a tumbling whore,
And, when he has done all his forced tricks, been glad
Of a poor spoonful of dead wine with flies in 't?
It cannot be. All his ingredients   105
Are a sheep's gall, a roasted bitch's marrow,
Some few sod earwigs, pounded caterpillars,
A little capon's grease, and fasting spittle.
I know 'em to a dram.

   Mosca.   I know not, sir,   110
But some on 't there they poured into his ears,
Some in his nostrils, and recovered him,
Applying but the fricace!

   Corv.   Pox o' that fricace!

   Mosca. And since, to seem the more officious   115
And flatt'ring of his health, there they have had,
At extreme fees, the college of physicians
Consulting on him how they might restore him;

100. VIRTUE: power.
102. OSTERIA: tavern.
107. SOD: stewed.
108. FASTING SPITTLE: spittle of a fasting person.
119. CATAPLASM: plaster.
132. DELATE: report.
147. QUEAN: strumpet.
150. MADE . . . IT: forced to it (not a professional).
153. GOD'S SO': God's soul.

Where one would have a cataplasm of spices,
Another a flayed ape clapped to his breast,   120
A third would ha' it a dog, a fourth an oil,
With wildcats' skins; at last, they all resolved
That to preserve him was no other means
But some young woman must be straight sought out,
Lusty and full of juice, to sleep by him.   125
And to this service, most unhappily
And most unwillingly, am I now employed;
Which here I thought to preacquaint you with,
For your advice, since it concerns you most,
Because I would not do that thing might cross   130
Your ends on whom I have my whole dependence, sir.
Yet, if I do it not, they may delate
My slackness to my patron, work me out
Of his opinion; and there all your hopes,
Ventures, or whatsoever, are all frustrate.   135
I do but tell you, sir. Besides, they are all
Now striving who shall first present him. Therefore—
I could entreat you, briefly, conclude somewhat;
Prevent 'em if you can.

   Corv.   Death to my hopes,   140
This is my villainous fortune! Best to hire
Some common courtesan.

   Mosca.   Ay, I thought on that, sir;
But they are all so subtle, full of art;
And age again doting and flexible,   145
So as—I cannot tell—we may perchance
Light on a quean may cheat us all.

   Corv.   'Tis true.

   Mosca. No, no. It must be one that has no tricks, sir,
Some simple thing, a creature made unto it;   150
Some wench you may command. Ha' you no
   kinswoman?
God's so'—Think, think, think, think, think, think,
   think, sir.
One o' the doctors offered there his daughter.   155

Corv. How!

Mosca.   Yes, Signor Lupo, the physician.

Corv. His daughter!

Mosca.   And a virgin, sir. Why, alas,
He knows the state of's body, what it is;   160
That nought can warm his blood, sir, but a fever;
Nor any incantation raise his spirit;
A long forgetfulness hath seized that part.
Besides, sir, who shall know it? Some one or two—

Corv. I pray thee give me leave.   [*Walks aside.*] 165
    If any man
But I had had this luck—The thing in 'tself,
I know, is nothing—Wherefore should not I
As well command my blood and my affections
As this dull doctor? In the point of honor,   170
The cases are all one, of wife and daughter.

Mosca. [*Aside*] I hear him coming.

Corv.   She shall do't. 'Tis done.
'Slight! If this doctor, who is not engaged,
Unless 't be for his counsel, which is nothing,   175
Offer his daughter, what should I, that am
So deeply in? I will prevent him. Wretch!
Covetous wretch!—Mosca, I have determined.

Mosca. How, sir?

Corv.   We'll make all sure. The party you wot of 180
Shall be mine own wife, Mosca.

Mosca.   Sir, the thing,
But that I would not seem to counsel you,
I should have motioned to you at the first;
And, make your count, you have cut all their throats. 185
Why, 'tis directly taking a possession!
And in his next fit we may let him go.

---

172. COMING: coming around to the idea.
174. 'SLIGHT: by God's light; ENGAGED: committed.
180. WOT: know.
184. MOTIONED: made a suggestion.
185. MAKE . . . COUNT: count upon it.
216. WILL: lust.
217. WATCHES: guards.

'Tis but to pull the pillow from his head
And he is throttled; 't had been done before,
But for your scrupulous doubts.   190
    Corv.   Ay, a plague on't,
My conscience fools my wit! Well, I'll be brief,
And so be thou, lest they should be before us.
Go home; prepare him; tell him with what zeal
And willingness I do it. Swear it was   195
On the first hearing—as thou mayst do, truly—
Mine own free motion.
    Mosca.   Sir, I warrant you,
I'll so possess him with it that the rest
Of his starved clients shall be banished all   200
And only you received. But come not, sir,
Until I send, for I have something else
To ripen for your good; you must not know't.
    Corv. But do not you forget to send now.
    Mosca.   Fear not.   205
                                [*Exit.*]

    Corv. Where are you, wife? My Celia! Wife!

[*Re-enter Celia.*]

                            What, blubbering?
Come, dry those tears. I think thou thoughtst me in
    earnest!
Ha! By this light, I talked so but to try thee.   210
Methinks the lightness of the occasion
Should ha' confirmed thee. Come, I am not jealous.
    Celia. No?
    Corv.   Faith I am not, I, nor never was;
It is a poor, unprofitable humor.   215
Do not I know, if women have a will,
They'll do 'gainst all the watches o' the world?
And that the fiercest spies are tamed with gold?
Tut, I am confident in thee, thou shalt see't;
And see, I'll give thee cause, too, to believe it.   220

Come kiss me. Go and make thee ready straight
In all thy best attire, thy choicest jewels,
Put 'em all on, and, with 'em, thy best looks.
We are invited to a solemn feast
At old Volpone's, where it shall appear   225
How far I am free from jealousy or fear.

[*Exeunt.*]

(III.ii)
2. PARTS: abilities.
5. WANTON: playful.
9. CLODPOLLS: blockheads.
10. MYSTERY: craft.
11. LIBERALLY PROFESSED: freely practiced.
20. FLEER: grin.
21. REVENUE: income; LEGS: bows; FACES: smiles.
22. LICK . . . MOTH: offer obsequious attentions.

ACT III

Scene I

[Enter Mosca.]

Mosca. I fear I shall begin to grow in love
With my dear self and my most prosp'rous parts,
They do so spring and burgeon. I can feel
A whimsy i' my blood; I know not how,
Success hath made me wanton. I could skip   5
Out of my skin now, like a subtle snake,
I am so limber. O, your parasite
Is a most precious thing, dropped from above,
Not bred 'mongst clods and clodpolls here on earth.
I muse the mystery was not made a science,   10
It is so liberally professed! Almost
All the wise world is little else, in nature,
But parasites or sub-parasites. And yet
I mean not those that have your bare town-art,
To know who's fit to feed 'em; have no house,   15
No family, no care, and therefore mold
Tales for men's ears, to bait that sense; or get
Kitchen invention and some stale receipts
To please the belly and the groin; nor those,
With their court-dog tricks, that can fawn and fleer, 20
Make their revenue out of legs and faces,
Echo my lord and lick away a moth;
But your fine, elegant rascal, that can rise
And stoop, almost together, like an arrow;
Shoot through the air as nimbly as a star;   25
Turn short as doth a swallow; and be here,
And there, and here, and yonder, all at once;

77

Present to any humor all occasion,
And change a visor swifter than a thought!
This is the creature had the art born with him;   30
Toils not to learn it but doth practice it
Out of most excellent nature; and such sparks
Are the true parasites, others but their zanies.

[*Enter Bonario.*]

Who's this? Bonario, old Corbaccio's son?
The person I was bound to seek. Fair sir,   35
You are happ'ly met.
    Bon.   That cannot be by thee.
    Mosca. Why, sir?
    Bon.   Nay, pray thee know thy way, and
        leave me.   40
I would be loath to interchange discourse
With such a mate as thou art.
    Mosca.   Courteous sir,
Scorn not my poverty.
    Bon.   Not I, by heaven!   45
But thou shalt give me leave to hate thy baseness.
    Mosca. Baseness?
    Bon.   Ay, answer me, is not thy sloth
Sufficient argument? Thy flattery?
Thy means of feeding?   50
    Mosca.   Heaven be good to me!
These imputations are too common, sir,

---

28. PRESENT . . . OCCASION: indulge any whim.
32. OUT . . . NATURE: naturally.
33. ZANIES: miserable imitators.
42. MATE: base fellow.
49. ARGUMENT: reason.
54. UNEQUAL: unfair.
62. CAREFUL: painfully earned.
64. FAIN: obliged.
65. OBSERVANCE: service.
69. MINING: undermining.
70. TRAINED: lured.
73. PROVE: try.
74. ESTIMATION: reputation.
76. PERSONATED: counterfeited.
80. MAIN: major.

And eas'ly stuck on virtue when she's poor;
You are unequal to me, and howe'er
Your sentence may be righteous, yet you are not   55
That, ere you know me, thus proceed in censure.
St. Mark bear witness 'gainst you, 'tis inhuman!
   Bon. [*Aside*] What! Does he weep? The sign is soft
    and good.
I do repent me that I was so harsh.   60
   Mosca. 'Tis true that, swayed by strong necessity,
I am enforced to eat my careful bread
With too much obsequy. 'Tis true, beside,
That I am fain to spin mine own poor raiment
Out of my mere observance, being not born   65
To a free fortune. But that I have done
Base offices, in rending friends asunder,
Dividing families, betraying counsels,
Whispering false lies, or mining men with praises,
Trained their credulity with perjuries,   70
Corrupted chastity, or am in love
With mine own tender ease; but would not rather
Prove the most rugged and laborious course
That might redeem my present estimation,
Let me here perish, in all hope of goodness!   75
   Bon. [*Aside*] This cannot be a personated passion.—
I was to blame so to mistake thy nature.
Pray thee forgive me and speak out thy business.
   Mosca. Sir, it concerns you; and though I may seem
At first to make a main offense in manners   80
And in my gratitude unto my master,
Yet, for the pure love which I bear all right
And hatred of the wrong, I must reveal it.
This very hour your father is in purpose
To disinherit you—   85
   Bon.   How!
   Mosca.   And thrust you forth,
As a mere stranger to his blood; 'tis true, sir.
The work no way engageth me but as

I claim an interest in the general state   90
Of goodness and true virtue, which I hear
T' abound in you; and for which mere respect,
Without a second aim, sir, I have done it.

   Bon. This tale hath lost thee much of the late trust
Thou hadst with me; it is impossible.   95
I know not how to lend it any thought
My father should be so unnatural.

   Mosca. It is a confidence that well becomes
Your piety; and formed, no doubt, it is
From your own simple innocence; which makes   100
Your wrong more monstrous and abhorred. But, sir,
I now will tell you more: this very minute
It is, or will be, doing; and if you
Shall be but pleased to go with me, I'll bring you—
I dare not say where you shall see—but where   105
Your ear shall be a witness of the deed;
Hear yourself written bastard and professed
The common issue of the earth.

   Bon.   I'm 'mazed!

   Mosca. Sir, if I do it not, draw your just sword   110
And score your vengeance on my front and face;
Mark me your villain. You have too much wrong,
And I do suffer for you, sir. My heart
Weeps blood in anguish—

   Bon.   Lead. I follow thee.   115

                           [Exeunt.]

---

92. RESPECT: consideration.
99. PIETY: filial loyalty.
108. COMMON . . . EARTH: of unknown antecedents.
111. FRONT: forehead.

(III.ii.)

5. WHETHER: which.
6. DELICATES: favorites.
13. EVERYTHING . . . PRETTY: proverbial.
18. FEAT: trim.
29. SEND . . . BE: grant that it be.

Scene [II]

[Enter Volpone.]

Volp. Mosca stays long, methinks.—Bring forth your
   sports
And help to make the wretched time more sweet.

[Enter Nano, Androgyno, and Castrone.]

Nano. Dwarf, fool, and eunuch, well met here we be.
A question it were now whether of us three,   5
Being all the known delicates of a rich man,
In pleasing him claim the precedency can?
   Cas. I claim for myself.
   And.   *And so doth the fool.*
   Nano. '*Tis foolish indeed. Let me set you both to* 10
   school:
First, for your dwarf, he's little and witty,
And everything, as it is little, is pretty;
Else why do men say to a creature of my shape
So soon as they see him, "It's a pretty little ape"?   15
And why a pretty ape but for pleasing imitation
Of greater men's action in a ridiculous fashion?
Beside, this feat body of mine doth not crave
Half the meat, drink, and cloth one of your bulks will
   have.   20
Admit your fool's face be the mother of laughter,
Yet, for his brain, it must always come after;
And though that do feed him, it's a pitiful case,
His body is beholding to such a bad face.
                            One knocks.
   Volp. Who's there? My couch! Away! Look!   25
     Nano, see!   *[Exeunt Androgyno and Castrone.]*
Give me my caps first—go, inquire.   *[Exit Nano.]*
   Now, Cupid
Send it be Mosca, and with fair return!

[*Re-enter Nano.*]

Nano. It is the beauteous Madam—   30
Volp.   Wouldbe—is it?
Nano. The same.
Volp.   Now torment on me! Squire her in;
For she will enter or dwell here forever.
Nay, quickly, that my fit were past. [*Exit Nano.*] I fear 35
A second hell, too, that my loathing this
Will quite expel my appetite to the other.
Would she were taking now her tedious leave.
Lord, how it threats me, what I am to suffer!

[*Re-enter Nano with Lady Wouldbe.*]

Lady. I thank you, good sir. Pray you signify   40
Unto your patron I am here. This band
Shows not my neck enough. I trouble you, sir;
Let me request you bid one of my women
Come hither to me. In good faith, I am dressed
Most favorably today! It is no matter;   45
'Tis well enough.

[*Enter 1st Woman.*]

                    Look, see these petulant things!
How they have done this!
Volp. [*Aside*]   I do feel the fever
Ent'ring in at mine ears. O for a charm   50
To fright it hence!
Lady.   Come nearer. Is this curl
In his right place, or this? Why is this higher
Than all the rest? You ha' not washed your eyes yet!

---

41. BAND: collar.
61. TIRE: headdress.
67. MUSE: wonder.
78. CURIOUS: fastidious.
83. FUCUS: cosmetic.

Or do they not stand even i' your head?   55
Where is your fellow? Call her.   [*Exit 1st Woman.*]
    Nano.   —Now, St. Mark
Deliver us! Anon she'll beat her women
Because her nose is red.

[*Re-enter 1st Woman with 2nd Woman.*]

    Lady.   I pray you, view   60
This tire, forsooth; are all things apt, or no?
    1. Wom. One hair a little here sticks out, forsooth.
    Lady. Does't so, forsooth? And where was your
        dear sight
When it did so, forsooth? What now! Bird-eyed?   65
And you, too? Pray you, both approach and mend it.
Now, by that light, I muse you're not ashamed!
I, that have preached these things so oft unto you,
Read you the principles, argued all the grounds,
Disputed every fitness, every grace,   70
Called you to counsel of so frequent dressings—
    Nano. [*Aside*] More carefully than of your fame or
        honor.
    Lady. Made you acquainted what an ample dowry
The knowledge of these things would be unto you,   75
Able alone to get you noble husbands
At your return; and you thus to neglect it!
Besides, you seeing what a curious nation
The Italians are, what will they say of me?
"The English lady cannot dress herself."   80
Here's a fine imputation to our country!
Well, go your ways, and stay i' the next room.
This fucus was too coarse, too; it's no matter.
Good sir, you'll give 'em entertainment?
                        [*Exit Nano with Women.*]
    Volp. The storm comes toward me.   85
    Lady.   How does my Volp!
    Volp. Troubled with noise, I cannot sleep; I dreamt

That a strange fury entered now my house,
And with the dreadful tempest of her breath
Did cleave my roof asunder.   90
   Lady.   Believe me, and I
Had the most fearful dream, could I remember't—
   Volp. [*Aside*] Out on my fate! I ha' giv'n her the
     occasion
How to torment me: she will tell me hers.   95
   Lady. Methought the golden mediocrity,
Polite and delicate—
   Volp.   O, if you do love me,
No more. I sweat and suffer at the mention
Of any dream. Feel how I tremble yet.   100
   Lady. Alas, good soul! The passion of the heart.
Seed pearl were good now, boiled with syrup of
    apples,
Tincture of gold, and coral, citron pills,
Your elecampane root, myrobalans—   105
   Volp. [*Aside*] Ay me, I have ta'en a grasshopper
    by the wing!
   Lady. Burnt silk and amber; you have muscatel
Good i' the house—
   Volp.   You will not drink and part?   110
   Lady. No, fear not that. I doubt we shall not get
Some English saffron—half a dram would serve—
Your sixteen cloves, a little musk, dried mints,
Bugloss, and barley meal—
   Volp. [*Aside*]   She's in again!   115
Before, I feigned diseases; now I have one.
   Lady. And these applied with a right scarlet cloth.

---

101. PASSION . . . HEART: heartburn.
110. PART: depart.
117. SCARLET CLOTH: red flannel is still regarded as having curative properties.
130. CONSENT: harmony.
133. POET: Sophocles in *Ajax*.
139. CIECO . . . HADRIA: "the blind man of Adria," Luigi Groto.
146. PASTOR FIDO: popular pastoral drama by Giovanni Battista Guarini.
150. HAPPY: fluent.
152. MONTAGNIÉ: Montaigne.

Volp. [*Aside*] Another flood of words! A very torrent!

Lady. Shall I, sir, make you a poultice?   120

Volp.   No, no, no!

I'm very well; you need prescribe no more.

   Lady. I have a little studied physic; but now

I'm all for music, save, i' the forenoons,

An hour or two for painting. I would have   125

A lady, indeed, t' have all letters and arts,

Be able to discourse, to write, to paint;

But principal, as Plato holds, your music—

And so does wise Pythagoras, I take it—

Is your true rapture; when there is consent   130

In face, in voice, and clothes; and is, indeed,

Our sex's chiefest ornament.

   Volp.   The poet

As old in time as Plato, and as knowing,

Says that your highest female grace is silence.   135

   Lady. Which o' your poets? Petrarch, or Tasso, or
   Dante?

Guarini? Ariosto? Aretine?

Cieco di Hadria? I have read them all.

   Volp. [*Aside*] Is everything a cause to my destruc- 140
   tion?

   Lady. I think I ha' two or three of 'em about me.

   Volp. [*Aside*] The sun, the sea, will sooner both
   stand still

Than her eternal tongue! Nothing can 'scape it.   145

   Lady. Here's *Pastor Fido*—

   Volp. [*Aside*]   Profess obstinate silence,

That's now my safest.

   Lady.   All our English writers,

I mean such as are happy in the Italian,   150

Will deign to steal out of this author mainly,

Almost as much as from Montagnié.

He has so modern and facile a vein,

Fitting the time, and catching the court ear.

\

Your Petrarch is more passionate, yet he,   155
In days of sonneting, trusted 'em with much.
Dante is hard, and few can understand him.
But, for a desperate wit, there's Aretine!
Only his pictures are a little obscene—
You mark me not.   160
     Volp.   Alas, my mind's perturbed.
     Lady. Why, in such cases we must cure ourselves,
Make use of our philosophy—
     Volp.   O'y me!
     Lady. And as we find our passions do rebel,   165
Encounter 'em with reason, or divert 'em,
By giving scope unto some other humor
Of lesser danger; as, in politic bodies,
There's nothing more doth overwhelm the judgment
And clouds the understanding than too much   170
Settling and fixing and, as 'twere, subsiding
Upon one object. For the incorporating
Of these same outward things into that part
Of which we call mental leaves some certain faeces
That stop the organs, and, as Plato says,   175
Assassinates our knowledge.
     Volp. [*Aside*]   Now, the spirit
Of patience help me!
     Lady.   Come, in faith, I must
Visit you more a-days, and make you well;   180
Laugh and be lusty!
     Volp. [*Aside*]   My good angel save me!
     Lady. There was but one sole man in all the world
With whom I e'er could sympathize; and he
Would lie you often three, four hours together   185
To hear me speak; and be sometime so rapt,

----

158. ARETINE: Pietro Aretino, noted for scurrilous and obscene writings.
164. O'Y ME: probably the Italian *ohimè* (alas).
174. FAECES: dregs.
193. COAETANEI: the same age.
211. PRESENTED: offered a gift.
217. TOY: trifle.

As he would answer me quite from the purpose,
Like you, and you are like him, just. I'll discourse,
An't be but only, sir, to bring you asleep,
How we did spend our time and loves together   190
For some six years.
   Volp.   O, O, O, O, O, O!
   Lady. For we were *coaetanei* and brought up—
   Volp. Some power, some fate, some fortune rescue
    me!   195

[*Enter Mosca.*]

   Mosca. God save you, madam!
   Lady.   Good sir.
   Volp.   Mosca! Welcome,
Welcome to my redemption.
   Mosca.   Why, sir?   200
   Volp.   O,
Rid me of this my torture quickly there,
My madam with the everlasting voice!
The bells, in time of pestilence, ne'er made
Like noise or were in that perpetual motion;   205
The cockpit comes not near it. All my house,
But now, steamed like a bath with her thick breath;
A lawyer could not have been heard; nor scarce
Another woman, such a hail of words
She has let fall. For hell's sake, rid her hence.   210
   Mosca. Has she presented?
   Volp.   O, I do not care!
I'll take her absence upon any price,
With any loss.
   Mosca.   Madam—   215
   Lady.   I ha' brought your patron
A toy, a cap here, of mine own work—
   Mosca.   'Tis well.
I had forgot to tell you I saw your knight
Where you'd little think it—   220

Lady.   Where?
Mosca.   Marry,
Where yet, if you make haste, you may apprehend him;
Rowing upon the water in a gondola,
With the most cunning courtesan of Venice.   225
    Lady. Is't true?
    Mosca.   Pursue 'em and believe your eyes.
Leave me to make your gift. [*Exit Lady Wouldbe
    hastily.*] I knew 'twould take.
For lightly they that use themselves most license   230
Are still most jealous.
    Volp.   Mosca, hearty thanks
For thy quick fiction and delivery of me.
Now, to my hopes, what sayst thou?

[*Re-enter Lady Wouldbe.*]

Lady.   But do you hear, sir? 235
Volp. Again! I fear a paroxysm.
    Lady.   Which way
Rowed they together?
    Mosca.   Toward the Rialto.
Lady. I pray you lend me your dwarf.   240
    Mosca.   I pray you take him.
                                [*Exit Lady Wouldbe.*]
Your hopes, sir, are like happy blossoms, fair,
And promise timely fruit, if you will stay
But the maturing. Keep you at your couch;
Corbaccio will arrive straight with the will.   245
When he is gone, I'll tell you more.   [*Exit.*]
    Volp.   My blood,
My spirits, are returned; I am alive.
And, like your wanton gamester at primero,

---

225. CUNNING: accomplished.
230. LIGHTLY: usually.
249. PRIMERO: a card game.

Whose thought had whispered to him, not go less,   250
Methinks I lie, and draw—for an encounter.
                   [*Closing the bed curtains.*]

[*Enter Mosca with Bonario.*]

   Mosca. Sir, here concealed, you may hear all. But
     pray you
Have patience, sir. (*One knocks.*) The same's your
     father knocks.   255
I am compelled to leave you.   [*Exit.*]
   Bon.   Do so. Yet
Cannot my thought imagine this a truth.
                   [*Conceals himself.*]

[*Enter Mosca, Corvino, followed by Celia.*]

   Mosca. Death on me! You are come too soon; what
     meant you?   260
Did not I say I would send?
   Corv.   Yes, but I feared
You might forget it, and then they prevent us.
   Mosca. [*Aside*] Prevent? Did e'er man haste so for
     his horns?   265
A courtier would not ply it so for a place.—
Well, now there's no helping it, stay here;
I'll presently return.   [*Exit.*]
   Corv.   Where are you, Celia?
You know not wherefore I have brought you hither?   270
   Celia. Not well, except you told me.
   Corv.   Now I will:
Hark hither.   [*Whispers to her.*]
   Mosca. [*To Bonario, concealed*] Sir, your father
     hath sent word   275
It will be half an hour ere he come.
And therefore, if you please to walk the while
Into that gallery—at the upper end

There are some books to entertain the time—
And I'll take care no man shall come unto you, sir.   280
   Bon. Yes, I will stay there. [*Aside*] I do doubt this
     fellow.   [*Exit.*]
   Mosca. There, he is far enough; he can hear nothing;
And for his father, I can keep him off.
              [*Withdraws to Volpone's couch.*]
   Corv. Nay, now there is no starting back, and there-   285
     fore,
Resolve upon it; I have so decreed.
It must be done. Nor would I move't afore,
Because I would avoid all shifts and tricks
That might deny me.   290
   Celia.   Sir, let me beseech you,
Affect not these strange trials. If you doubt
My chastity, why, lock me up forever;
Make me the heir of darkness. Let me live
Where I may please your fears, if not your trust.   295
   Corv. Believe it, I have no such humor, I.
All that I speak I mean; yet I am not mad,
Not horn-mad, see you? Go to, show yourself
Obedient and a wife.
   Celia.   O heaven!   300
   Corv.   I say it,
Do so.
   Celia. Was this the train?
   Corv.   I've told you reasons:
What the physicians have set down, how much   305
It may concern me, what my engagements are,
My means, and the necessity of those means

---

288. MOVE'T: suggest it.
298. GO TO: come on.
303. TRAIN: stratagem.
306. ENGAGEMENTS: obligations.
311. BREATH: word.
322. FAME: reputation.
323. JIG: joke.
339. CONNED: studied; PRINTS: obscene designs accompanied Aretino's *Sonnetti lussuriosi.*
341. CRITIC: connoisseur.

For my recovery. Wherefore, if you be
Loyal and mine, be won, respect my venture.
   Celia. Before your honor?   310
   Corv.   Honor! Tut, a breath;
There's no such thing in nature: a mere term
Invented to awe fools. What is my gold
The worse for touching? Clothes for being looked on?
Why, this 's no more. An old, decrepit wretch   315
That has no sense, no sinew; takes his meat
With others' fingers; only knows to gape
When you do scald his gums; a voice, a shadow;
And what can this man hurt you?
   Celia. [*Aside*]   Lord! What spirit   320
Is this hath entered him?
   Corv.   And for your fame,
That's such a jig; as if I would go tell it,
Cry it on the Piazza! Who shall know it,
But he that cannot speak it and this fellow,   325
Whose lips are i' my pocket, save yourself?
If you'll proclaim't, you may. I know no other
Should come to know it.
   Celia.   Are heaven and saints then
       nothing?   330
Will they be blind or stupid?
   Corv.   How?
   Celia.   Good sir,
Be jealous still, emulate them; and think
What hate they burn with toward every sin.   335
   Corv. I grant you. If I thought it were a sin,
I would not urge you. Should I offer this
To some young Frenchman or hot Tuscan blood,
That had read Aretine, conned all his prints,
Knew every quirk within lust's labyrinth,   340
And were professed critic in lechery;
And I would look upon him and applaud him—
This were a sin. But here 'tis contrary:

A pious work, mere charity, for physic,
And honest polity to assure mine own.   345

   Celia. O heaven! Canst thou suffer such a change?

   Volp. Thou art mine honor, Mosca, and my pride,
My joy, my tickling, my delight! Go bring 'em.

   Mosca. Please you draw near, sir.

   Corv.   Come on, what— 350
You will not be rebellious? By that light—

   Mosca. Sir, Signor Corvino here is come to see you.

   Volp. O!

   Mosca. And hearing of the consultation had,
So lately, for your health, is come to offer,   355
Or rather, sir, to prostitute—

   Corv.   Thanks, sweet Mosca.

   Mosca. Freely, unasked, or unentreated—

   Corv.   Well!

   Mosca. As the true, fervent instance of his love, 360
His own most fair and proper wife, the beauty
Only of price in Venice—

   Corv.   'Tis well urged.

   Mosca. To be your comfortress, and to preserve you.

   Volp. Alas, I am past already! Pray you thank him 365
For his good care and promptness; but for that,
'Tis a vain labor e'en to fight 'gainst heaven,
Applying fire to stone—uh, uh, uh, uh!—
Making a dead leaf grow again. I take
His wishes gently, though; and you may tell him 370
What I've done for him. Marry, my state is hopeless!
Will him to pray for me and t' use his fortune
With reverence when he comes to 't.

   Mosca.   Do you hear, sir?
Go to him with your wife.   375

---

345. POLITY: strategy.
362. ONLY . . . PRICE: of highest price.
386. ROCHET: red gurnet.
387. DEATH: God's death!
391. AQUA FORTIS: nitric acid.
392. CORSIVES: corrosives.
403. BE ADVISED: be wise and do as you are told.
409. ARRANT LOCUST: downright plague.

Corv.   Heart of my father!
Wilt thou persist thus? Come, I pray thee, come.
Thou seest 'tis nothing, Celia. By this hand,
I shall grow violent. Come, do't, I say.

   Celia. Sir, kill me rather. I will take down poison, 380
Eat burning coals, do anything—

   Corv.   Be damned!
Heart, I will drag thee hence home by the hair,
Cry thee a strumpet through the streets, rip up
Thy mouth unto thine ears, and slit thy nose   385
Like a raw rochet—Do not tempt me, come!
Yield, I am loath—Death! I will buy some slave,
Whom I will kill and bind thee to him alive,
And at my window hang you forth; devising
Some monstrous crime, which I, in capital letters,   390
Will eat into thy flesh with aqua fortis
And burning corsives on this stubborn breast.
Now, by the blood thou has incensed, I'll do't!

   Celia. Sir, what you please you may; I am your
     martyr.   395

   Corv. Be not thus obstinate; I ha' not deserved it.
Think who it is entreats you. Pray thee, sweet—
Good faith, thou shalt have jewels, gowns, attires,
What thou wilt think and ask. Do but go kiss him.
Or touch him but. For my sake. At my suit.   400
This once. No? Not? I shall remember this!
Will you disgrace me thus? D'you thirst my undoing?

   Mosca. Nay, gentle lady, be advised.

   Corv.   No, no.
She has watched her time. God's precious, this is 405
     scurvy,
'Tis very scurvy; and you are—

   Mosca.   Nay, good sir.

   Corv. An arrant locust, by heaven, a locust! Whore,
Crocodile, that hast thy tears prepared,   410
Expecting how thou'lt bid 'em flow.

Mosca.   Nay, pray you, sir,
She will consider.
    Celia.   Would my life would serve
To satisfy.   415
    Corv. 'Sdeath! If she would but speak to him,
And save my reputation, 'twere somewhat;
But spitefully to affect my utter ruin!
    Mosca. Ay, now you've put your fortune in her
        hands.   420
Why, i'faith, it is her modesty; I must quit her.
If you were absent, she would be more coming;
I know it, and dare undertake for her.
What woman can before her husband! Pray you,
Let us depart and leave her here.   425
    Corv.   Sweet Celia,
Thou mayst redeem all yet; I'll say no more.
If not, esteem yourself as lost. Nay, stay here.
                            [*Exit with Mosca.*]
    Celia. O God and his good angels! Whither, whither
Is shame fled human breasts, that with such ease   430
Men dare put off your honors and their own?
Is that which ever was a cause of life
Now placed beneath the basest circumstance,
And modesty an exile made, for money?
    Volp. (*Leaps off from his couch*) Ay, in Corvino 435
        and such earth-fed minds,
That never tasted the true heav'n of love.
Assure thee, Celia, he that would sell thee
Only for hope of gain, and that uncertain,

---

418. AFFECT: prefer.
421. QUIT: justify.
422. COMING: acquiescent.
423. UNDERTAKE: vouch.
441. COPEMAN: chapman; merchant.
448. PRACTICE: scheming.
450. PROTEUS: a sea-god who had the power to assume any shape;
HORNED FLOOD: Achelous, a river-god, who fought Hercules in the
form of a bull.
460. VALOIS: Henry, Duke of Anjou, later Henry III of France.
461. ANTINOUS: handsome favorite of the Emperor Hadrian.
463. NOTE: characteristic.
464. PROVE: try.

He would have sold his part of paradise   440
For ready money, had he met a copeman.
Why art thou 'mazed to see me thus revived?
Rather applaud thy beauty's miracle;
'Tis thy great work that hath, not now alone
But sundry times, raised me in several shapes,   445
And, but this morning, like a mountebank,
To see thee at thy window. Ay, before
I would have left my practice for thy love,
In varying figures I would have contended
With the blue Proteus or the horned flood.   450
Now art thou welcome.
   Celia.   Sir!
   Volp.   Nay, fly me not.
Nor let thy false imagination
That I was bedrid make thee think I am so.   455
Thou shalt not find it. I am now as fresh,
As hot, as high, and in as jovial plight,
As when, in that so celebrated scene
At recitation of our comedy
For entertainment of the great Valois,   460
I acted young Antinous and attracted
The eyes and ears of all the ladies present,
T' admire each graceful gesture, note, and footing.

Song.

     Come, my Celia, let us prove,
     While we can, the sports of love.   465
     Time will not be ours forever,
     He at length our good will sever;
     Spend not then his gifts in vain.
     Suns that set may rise again;
     But if once we lose this light,   470
     'Tis with us perpetual night.
     Why should we defer our joys?
     Fame and rumor are but toys.

Cannot we delude the eyes
Of a few poor household spies?   475
Or his easier ears beguile,
Thus removed by our wile?
'Tis no sin love's fruits to steal,
But the sweet thefts to reveal:
To be taken, to be seen,   480
These have crimes accounted been.

Celia. Some serene blast me, or dire lightning strike
This my offending face.
  Volp.   Why droops my Celia?
Thou hast, in place of a base husband, found   485
A worthy lover; use thy fortune well,
With secrecy and pleasure. See, behold
What thou art queen of, not in expectation—
As I feed others—but possessed and crowned.
See, here, a rope of pearl, and each more orient   490
Than that the brave Egyptian queen caroused—
Dissolve and drink 'em. See, a carbuncle
May put out both the eyes of our St. Mark;
A diamond would have bought Lollia Paulina,
When she came in like starlight, hid with jewels   495
That were the spoils of provinces—take these
And wear, and lose 'em, yet remains an earring
To purchase them again and this whole state.

482. SERENE: tropical evening mist, regarded as infectious.
491. BRAVE: splendid; CAROUSED: drank. Cleopatra was reported to
have drunk dissolved pearls.
494. LOLLIA PAULINA: Pliny described the splendid jewels she wore
during her brief marriage to the Emperor Caligula.
502. ESTRICHES: ostriches.
503. PHOENIX: legendary bird that existed in only one specimen.
504. THOUGH . . . DISH: i.e., we would dine on the phoenix though
it meant the extinction of the species.
514. JULYFLOWERS: gillyflowers.
516. PANTHERS' BREATH: medieval bestiaries described the panther's
breath as smelling like allspice.
519. ROOF: head.
521. ANTIC: comic interlude.
522. OVID'S TALES: the *Metamorphoses*.
523. EUROPA: nymph carried off by Jove in the form of a bull.
524. ERYCINA: Sicilian name for Venus.
530. SOPHY: Shah.
531. GRAND SIGNOR: Sultan of Turkey.
533. QUICK: lively.

A gem but worth a private patrimony
Is nothing; we will eat such at a meal.   500
The heads of parrots, tongues of nightingales,
The brains of peacocks and of estriches
Shall be our food; and, could we get the phoenix,
Though nature lost her kind, she were our dish.
   Celia. Good sir, these things might move a mind 505
    affected
With such delights; but I, whose innocence
Is all I can think wealthy or worth the enjoying,
And which, once lost, I have nought to lose beyond it,
Cannot be taken with these sensual baits.   510
If you have conscience—
   Volp.   'Tis the beggar's virtue.
If thou hast wisdom, hear me, Celia.
Thy baths shall be the juice of Julyflowers,
Spirit of roses and of violets,   515
The milk of unicorns, and panthers' breath
Gathered in bags and mixed with Cretan wines.
Our drink shall be prepared gold and amber,
Which we will take until my roof whirl round
With the vertigo; and my dwarf shall dance,   520
My eunuch sing, my fool make up the antic.
Whilst we, in changed shapes, act Ovid's tales,
Thou like Europa, now, and I like Jove,
Then I like Mars and thou like Erycina;
So of the rest, till we have quite run through   525
And wearied all the fables of the gods.
Then will I have thee in more modern forms,
Attired like some sprightly dame of France,
Brave Tuscan lady, or proud Spanish beauty;
Sometimes unto the Persian Sophy's wife,   530
Or the Grand Signor's mistress; and for change,
To one of our most artful courtesans,
Or some quick Negro or cold Russian.
And I will meet thee in as many shapes;

Where we may so transfuse our wand'ring souls   535
Out at our lips and score up sums of pleasures,

      That the curious shall not know
      How to tell them as they flow;
      And the envious, when they find
      What their number is, be pined.   540

   Celia. If you have ears that will be pierced, or eyes
That can be opened, a heart may be touched,
Or any part that yet sounds man about you;
If you have touch of holy saints or heaven,
Do me the grace to let me 'scape. If not,   545
Be bountiful and kill me. You do know
I am a creature hither ill betrayed
By one whose shame I would forget it were.
If you will deign me neither of these graces,
Yet feed your wrath, sir, rather than your lust—   550
It is a vice comes nearer manliness—
And punish that unhappy crime of nature
Which you miscall my beauty. Flay my face,
Or poison it with ointments, for seducing
Your blood to this rebellion. Rub these hands   555
With what may cause an eating leprosy
E'en to my bones and marrow—anything
That may disfavor me, save in my honor.
And I will kneel to you, pray for you, pay down
A thousand hourly vows, sir, for your health;   560
Report and think you virtuous—
   Volp.   Think me cold,
Frozen, and impotent, and so report me?
That I had Nestor's hernia thou wouldst think.
I do degenerate and abuse my nation   565

---

537. CURIOUS: closely observant.
538. TELL: count.
540. PINED: racked with envious longing.
558. DISFAVOR: disfigure.
582. UNSPIRITED: dejected.
593. ENGAGED: imperiled.

To play with opportunity thus long.
I should have done the act and then have parleyed.
Yield, or I'll force thee.
   Celia.   O just God!
   Volp.   In vain—   570
   Bon. (*Leaps out from where Mosca had placed him*)
      Forbear, foul ravisher! Libidinous swine!
Free the forced lady or thou diest, impostor.
But that I am loath to snatch thy punishment
Out of the hand of justice, thou shouldst yet
Be made the timely sacrifice of vengeance,   575
Before this altar and this dross, thy idol.
Lady, let's quit the place; it is the den
Of villainy. Fear nought, you have a guard;
And he ere long shall meet his just reward.
                  [*Exeunt Bonario and Celia.*]
   Volp. Fall on me, roof, and bury me in ruin!   580
Become my grave that wert my shelter! O!
I am unmasked, unspirited, undone,
Betrayed to beggary, to infamy—

        [*Enter Mosca, wounded.*]

   Mosca. Where shall I run, most wretched shame of
    men,   585
To beat out my unlucky brains?
   Volp.   Here, here.
What! Dost thou bleed?
   Mosca.   O that his well-driv'n sword
Had been so courteous to have cleft me down   590
Unto the navel ere I lived to see
My life, my hopes, my spirits, my patron, all
Thus desperately engaged by my error.
   Volp. Woe on thy fortune.
   Mosca.   And my follies, sir.   595
   Volp. Th'ast made me miserable.
   Mosca.   And myself, sir.

Who would have thought he would have hearkened
   so?

  Volp. What shall we do?   600

    Mosca.   I know not; if my heart
Could expiate the mischance, I'ld pluck it out.
Will you be pleased to hang me, or cut my throat?
And I'll requite you, sir. Let's die like Romans,
Since we have lived like Grecians.   605

                          They knock without.

  Volp.   Hark! Who's there?
I hear some footing; officers, the *Saffi*,
Come to apprehend us! I do feel the brand
Hissing already at my forehead; now
Mine ears are boring.   610

    Mosca.   To your couch, sir; you
Make that place good, however. [*Volpone lies down
    as before.*] Guilty men
Suspect what they deserve still. Signor Corbaccio!

[*Enter Corbaccio.*]

  Corb. Why, how now, Mosca?   615

    Mosca.   O, undone, amazed, sir!
Your son—I know not by what accident—
Acquainted with your purpose to my patron,
Touching your will and making him your heir,
Entered our house with violence, his sword drawn,   620
Sought for you, called you wretch, unnatural,
Vowed he would kill you.

    Corb.   Me?

    Mosca.   Yes, and my patron.

---

604. REQUITE: repay in kind.
605. GRECIANS: proverbially given to riotous living.
607. SAFFI: Venetian police officials.
610. BORING: being bored.
612. HOWEVER: at least.
629. CAREFUL: solicitous.
631. TENDERED: tenderly regarded.
654. FOISTS: (1) roguish tricks; (2) fusty smells.

Corb. This act shall disinherit him indeed!   625
Here is the will.

    Mosca.   'Tis well, sir.

    Corb.   Right and well.
Be you as careful now for me.

[*Enter Voltore, behind*.]

    Mosca.   My life, sir,   630
Is not more tendered; I am only yours.

    Corb. How does he? Will he die shortly, thinkst
    thou?

    Mosca. I fear
He'll outlast May.   635

    Corb.   Today?

    Mosca.   No, last out May, sir.

    Corb. Couldst thou not gi' him a dram?

    Mosca.   O, by no means, sir!

    Corb. Nay, I'll not bid you.   640

    Volt.   This is a knave, I see.

    Mosca. [*Aside*] How! Signor Voltore! Did he hear
    me?

    Volt. Parasite!

    Mosca. Who's that? O sir, most timely welcome—   645

    Volt.   Scarce,
To the discovery of your tricks, I fear.
You are his only? And mine also, are you not?

    Mosca. Who? I, sir!

    Volt.   You, sir. What device is this   650
About a will?

    Mosca.   A plot for you, sir.

    Volt.   Come,
Put not your foists upon me; I shall scent 'em.

    Mosca. Did you not hear it?   655

    Volt.   Yes, I hear Corbaccio
Hath made your patron there his heir.

    Mosca.   'Tis true;

By my device, drawn to it by my plot,
With hope—   660
    Volt.   Your patron should reciprocate?
And you have promised?
    Mosca.   For your good I did, sir.
Nay, more, I told his son, brought, hid him here,
Where he might hear his father pass the deed;   665
Being persuaded to it by his thought, sir:
That the unnaturalness, first, of the act,
And then his father's oft disclaiming in him—
Which I did mean t'help on—would sure enrage him
To do some violence upon his parent;   670
On which the law should take sufficient hold,
And you be stated in a double hope.
Truth be my comfort and my conscience,
My only aim was to dig you a fortune
Out of these two old rotten sepulchers—   675
    Volt. I cry thee mercy, Mosca.
    Mosca.   Worth your patience
And your great merit, sir. And see the change!
    Volt. Why, what success?
    Mosca.   Most hapless! You must help, sir.   680
Whilst we expected the old raven, in comes
Corvino's wife, sent hither by her husband—
    Volt. What, with a present?
    Mosca.   No, sir, on visitation—
I'll tell you how anon—and, staying long,   685
The youth he grows impatient, rushes forth,
Seizeth the lady, wounds me, makes her swear—
Or he would murder her, that was his vow—
T'affirm my patron to have done her rape;
Which how unlike it is you see! And hence   690
With that pretext he's gone, t' accuse his father,
Defame my patron, defeat you—

---

668. DISCLAIMING IN: disowning of.
672. STATED: settled.
696. SCRUTINEO: senate house.

Volt.   Where's her husband?
Let him be sent for straight.
  Mosca.   Sir, I'll go fetch him.   695
  Volt. Bring him to the *Scrutineo.*
  Mosca.   Sir, I will.
  Volt. This must be stopped.
  Mosca.   O, you do nobly, sir.
Alas, 'twas labored all, sir, for your good;   700
Nor was there want of counsel in the plot.
But fortune can, at any time, o'erthrow
The projects of a hundred learned clerks, sir.
  Corb. What's that?
  Volt.   Will't please you, sir, to go along? 705
        [Exit Voltore, followed by Corbaccio.]
  Mosca. Patron, go in and pray for our success.
  Volp. Need makes devotion. Heaven your labor
    bless!
                       [Exeunt.]

ACT IV

Scene I

[Enter Sir Politic Wouldbe and Peregrine.]

Sir Pol. I told you, sir, it was a plot. You see
What observation is. You mentioned me
For some instructions: I will tell you, sir,
Since we are met here in this height of Venice,
Some few particulars I have set down,   5
Only for this meridian, fit to be known
Of your crude traveler; and they are these.
I will not touch, sir, at your phrase or clothes,
For they are old.

    Per.   Sir, I have better.   10

    Sir Pol.   Pardon,
I meant, as they are themes.

    Per.   O sir, proceed.
I'll slander you no more of wit, good sir.

    Sir Pol. First, for your garb, it must be grave and   15
        serious,
Very reserved and locked; not tell a secret
On any terms, not to your father; scarce
A fable but with caution; make sure choice

(IV.i.)
2. MENTIONED: asked.
12. THEMES: subjects of discourse.
15. GARB: manner.
25. KNOW: recognize.
26. BE . . . 'EM: keep their friendship.
32. BODIN: Jean Bodin, author of a well-known treatise on political science.
41. PREPOSTEROUS: going against custom; HAS HIM: knows his character.
48. CONTARINI: Cardinal Gasparo Contarini, *La republica e i magistrati di Vinegia* (1544); an English translation appeared in 1599.
55. THINK: worry.

Both of your company and discourse; beware   20
You never speak a truth—
  Per.   How?
  Sir Pol.   Not to strangers,
For those be they you must converse with most;
Others I would not know, sir, but at distance,   25
So as I still might be a saver in 'em;
You shall have tricks else passed upon you hourly.
And then, for your religion, profess none,
But wonder at the diversity of all;
And, for your part, protest were there no other   30
But simply the laws o' the land you could content you.
Nick Machiavel and Monsieur Bodin both
Were of this mind. Then must you learn the use
And handling of your silver fork at meals,
The metal of your glass—these are main matters   35
With your Italian—and to know the hour
When you must eat your melons and your figs.
  Per. Is that a point of state, too?
  Sir Pol.   Here it is.
For your Venetian, if he see a man   40
Preposterous in the least, he has him straight.
He has; he strips him. I'll acquaint you, sir,
I now have lived here 'tis some fourteen months;
Within the first week of my landing here,
All took me for a citizen of Venice.   45
I knew the forms so well—
  Per. [*Aside*]   And nothing else.
  Sir Pol. I had read Contarini, took me a house,
Dealt with my Jews to furnish it with movables—
Well, if I could but find one man, one man   50
To mine own heart, whom I durst trust, I would—
  Per. What, what, sir?
  Sir Pol.   Make him rich; make him a
   fortune.
He should not think again. I would command it.   55
  Per. As how?

Sir Pol.   With certain projects that I have,
Which I may not discover.

Per. [*Aside*]   If I had
But one to wager with, I would lay odds now   60
He tells me instantly.

Sir Pol.   One is—and that
I care not greatly who knows—to serve the state
Of Venice with red herrings for three years,
And at a certain rate, from Rotterdam,   65
Where I have correspondence. There's a letter,
Sent me from one o' the States and to that purpose.
He cannot write his name, but that's his mark.

Per. He is a chandler?

Sir Pol.   No, a cheesemonger.   70
There are some other, too, with whom I treat
About the same negotiation;
And I will undertake it. For 'tis thus:
I'll do't with ease, I've cast it all. Your hoy
Carries but three men in her and a boy,   75
And she shall make me three returns a year;
So if there come but one of three, I save;
If two, I can defalk. But this is, now,
If my main project fail.

Per.   Then you have others?   80

Sir Pol. I should be loath to draw the subtle air
Of such a place without my thousand aims.
I'll not dissemble, sir, where'er I come,
I love to be considerative; and 'tis true
I have at my free hours thought upon   85
Some certain goods unto the state of Venice,
Which I do call my cautions; and, sir, which
I mean, in hope of pension, to propound

---

58. DISCOVER: reveal.
67. STATES: States-General of the Low Countries.
69. CHANDLER: dealer in candles.
74. CAST: calculated; HOY: small sailing vessel.
78. DEFALK: cut back expenses.
84. CONSIDERATIVE: prudent.
101. GENTRY: good breeding.
111. PUT CASE: just suppose.

To the Great Council, then unto the Forty,
So to the Ten. My means are made already—   90
  Per. By whom?
  Sir Pol.   Sir, one that though his place be obscure,
Yet he can sway, and they will hear him. He's
A *commandadore.*   95
  Per.   What! A common sergeant?
  Sir Pol. Sir, such as they are put it in their mouths
What they should say, sometimes, as well as greater.
I think I have my notes to show you—
  Per.   Good, sir.   100
  Sir Pol. But you shall swear unto me, on your gentry,
Not to anticipate—
  Per.   I, sir?
  Sir Pol.   Nor reveal
A circumstance—My paper is not with me.   105
  Per. O, but you can remember, sir.
  Sir Pol.   My first is
Concerning tinderboxes. You must know,
No family is here without its box.
Now, sir, it being so portable a thing,   110
Put case that you or I were ill affected
Unto the state; sir, with it in our pockets,
Might not I go into the Arsenal?
Or you? Come out again? And none the wiser?
  Per. Except yourself, sir.   115
  Sir Pol.   Go to, then. I therefore
Advertise to the state how fit it were
That none but such as were known patriots,
Sound lovers of their country, should be suffered
T' enjoy them in their houses; and even those   120
Sealed at some office, and at such a bigness
As might not lurk in pockets.
  Per.   Admirable!
  Sir Pol. My next is how t' inquire, and be resolved
By present demonstration, whether a ship,   125

Newly arrived from Soria, or from
Any suspected part of all the Levant,
Be guilty of the plague. And, where they use
To lie out forty, fifty days, sometimes,
About the *Lazaretto* for their trial;   130
I'll save that charge and loss unto the merchant,
And in an hour clear the doubt.

  Per.   Indeed, sir!

  Sir Pol. Or—I will lose my labor.

  Per.   My faith, that's much. 135

  Sir Pol. Nay, sir, conceive me. 'Twill cost me, in
   onions,
Some thirty livres—

  Per.   Which is one pound sterling.

  Sir Pol. Beside my waterworks. For this I do, sir: 140
First, I bring in your ship 'twixt two brick walls—
But those the state shall venture. On the one
I strain me a fair tarpaulin and in that
I stick my onions, cut in halves; the other
Is full of loopholes, out at which I thrust   145
The noses of my bellows; and those bellows
I keep, with waterworks, in perpetual motion,
Which is the easiest matter of a hundred.
Now, sir, your onion, which doth naturally
Attract the infection, and your bellows blowing   150
The air upon him, will show instantly,
By his changed color, if there be contagion;
Or else remain as fair as at the first.
Now 'tis known, 'tis nothing.

  Per.   You are right, sir.   155

  Sir Pol. I would I had my note.

---

126. SORIA: Syria.
130. LAZARETTO: quarantine area.
143. STRAIN: stretch.
151. HIM: it.
176. RAGION . . . STATO: state affairs.
179. CHEAPENED: bargained for.
181. SLIP: neglect.
182. QUOTE: make note of.
188. BOTH: i.e., fast and loose.

Per.   Faith, so would I.
But you ha' done well for once, sir.
　　Sir Pol.   Were I false,
Or would be made so, I could show you reasons   160
How I could sell this state now to the Turk,
Spite of their galleys or their—
　　Per.   Pray you, Sir Poll.
　　Sir Pol. I have 'em not about me.
　　Per.   That I feared.   165
They're there, sir?
　　Sir Pol.   No, this is my diary,
Wherein I note my actions of the day.
　　Per. Pray you let's see, sir. What is here?—
　　"*Notandum.*   170
A rat had gnawn my spur leathers; notwithstanding,
I put on new and did go forth; but first
I threw three beans over the threshold. Item,
I went and bought two toothpicks, whereof one
I burst immediately in a discourse   175
With a Dutch merchant 'bout *ragion del stato.*
From him I went and paid a *muccinigo*
For piecing my silk stockings; by the way
I cheapened sprats; and at St. Mark's I urined."
Faith these are politic notes!   180
　　Sir Pol.   Sir, I do slip
No action of my life, thus, but I quote it.
　　Per. Believe me, it is wise!
　　Sir Pol.   Nay, sir, read forth.

[*Enter Lady Wouldbe, Nano, and Two Women.*]

Lady. Where should this loose knight be, trow?   185
　　Sure, he's housed.
Nano. Why, then he's fast.
Lady.   Ay, he plays both with me.
I pray you stay. This heat will do more harm
To my complexion than his heart is worth.   190

I do not care to hinder but to take him.
How it comes off!

   1. Wom. My master's yonder.

   Lady.   Where?

   2. Wom. With a young gentleman.   195

   Lady.   That same's the party,
In man's apparel! Pray you, sir, jog my knight.
I will be tender to his reputation,
However he demerit.

   Sir Pol.   My lady!   200

   Per.   Where?

   Sir Pol. 'Tis she indeed, sir, you shall know her. She
   is,
Were she not mine, a lady of that merit,
For fashion and behavior; and for beauty   205
I durst compare—

   Per.   It seems you are not jealous,
That dare commend her.

   Sir Pol.   Nay, and for discourse—

   Per. Being your wife, she cannot miss that.   210

   Sir Pol.   Madam,
Here is a gentleman, pray you use him fairly;
He seems a youth, but he is—

   Lady.   None?

   Sir Pol.   Yes, one   215
Has put his face as soon into the world—

   Lady. You mean, as early? But today?

   Sir Pol.   How's this?

   Lady. Why, in this habit, sir, you apprehend me.
Well, Master Wouldbe, this doth not become you.   220
I had thought the odor, sir, of your good name

Had been more precious to you; that you would not
Have done this dire massacre on your honor;
One of your gravity, and rank besides!
But knights, I see, care little for the oath   225
They make to ladies, chiefly their own ladies.
   Sir Pol. Now, by my spurs, the symbol of my knight-
     hood—
   Per. [*Aside*] Lord, how his brain is humbled for an
     oath!   230
   Sir Pol. I reach you not.
   Lady.   Right, sir, your polity
May bear it through thus. [*To Peregrine*] Sir, a word
     with you.
I would be loath to contest publicly   235
With any gentlewoman, or to seem
Froward, or violent, as *The Courtier* says—
It comes too near rusticity in a lady,
Which I would shun by all means. And however
I may deserve from Master Wouldbe, yet   240
T' have one fair gentlewoman thus be made
The unkind instrument to wrong another,
And one she knows not, ay, and to persever,
In my poor judgment is not warranted
From being a solecism in our sex,   245
If not in manners.
   Per.   How is this!
   Sir Pol.   Sweet madam,
Come nearer to your aim.
   Lady.   Marry and will, sir.   250
Since you provoke me with your impudence
And laughter of your light land-siren here,
Your Sporus, your hermaphrodite—
   Per.   What's here?
Poetic fury and historic storms!   255
   Sir Pol. The gentleman, believe it, is of worth
And of our nation.
   Lady. Ay, your Whitefriars nation!

Come, I blush for you, Master Wouldbe, I;
And am ashamed you should ha' no more forehead   260
Than thus to be the patron, or St. George,
To a lewd harlot, a base fricatrice,
A female devil in a male outside.
    Sir Pol.   Nay,
And you be such a one, I must bid adieu   265
To your delights. The case appears too liquid. [*Exit.*]
    Lady. Ay, you may carry 't clear, with your state
          face!
But for your carnival concupiscence,
Who here is fled for liberty of conscience   270
From furious persecution of the Marshal,
Her will I disc'ple.
    Per.   This is fine, i' faith!
And do you use this often? Is this part
Of your wit's exercise, 'gainst you have occasion?   275
Madam—
    Lady. Go to, sir.
    Per.   Do you hear me, lady?
Why, if your knight have set you to beg shirts,
Or to invite me home, you might have done it   280
A nearer way by far.
    Lady.   This cannot work you
Out of my snare.
    Per.   Why, am I in it, then?
Indeed your husband told me you were fair,   285
And so you are; only your nose inclines—
That side that's next the sun—to the queen apple.
    Lady. This cannot be endured by any patience.

---

260. FOREHEAD: sense of shame.
262. FRICATRICE: whore.
266. LIQUID: transparent.
267. CARRY 'T CLEAR: pretend innocence.
267-68. STATE FACE: solemn expression.
272. DISC'PLE: discipline.
275. 'GAINST: when.
281. A . . . WAY: more directly.
294. CALLET: strumpet.
319. FRESHMANSHIP: inexperience; SALT HEAD: seasoned judgment
(with a pun on "salt" as the opposite of "fresh").

[*Enter Mosca.*]

Mosca. What's the matter, madam?
Lady.   If the Senate   290
Right not my quest in this, I will protest 'em
To all the world no aristocracy.
    Mosca. What is the injury, lady?
    Lady.   Why, the callet
You told me of here I have ta'en disguised.   295
    Mosca. Who? This! What means your ladyship?
        The creature
I mentioned to you is apprehended now
Before the Senate. You shall see her—
    Lady.   Where?   300
    Mosca. I'll bring you to her. This young gentleman,
I saw him land this morning at the port.
    Lady. Is't possible? How has my judgment wan-
        dered!
Sir, I must, blushing, say to you I have erred,   305
And plead your pardon.
    Per.   What, more changes yet?
    Lady. I hope y' ha' not the malice to remember
A gentlewoman's passion. If you stay
In Venice here, please you to use me, sir—   310
    Mosca. Will you go, madam?
    Lady.   Pray you, sir, use me. In faith,
The more you see me, the more I shall conceive
You have forgot our quarrel.
            [*Exeunt Lady Wouldbe, Mosca, Nano, and
                            Women.*]
    Per.   This is rare!   315
Sir Politic Wouldbe? No, Sir Politic Bawd,
To bring me thus acquainted with his wife!
Well, wise Sir Poll, since you have practiced thus
Upon my freshmanship, I'll try your salt head,
What proof it is against a counterplot.   320
            [*Exit.*]

Scene [II]

[*Enter Voltore, Corbaccio, Corvino, and Mosca.*]

Volt. Well, now you know the carriage of the
   business,
Your constancy is all that is required
Unto the safety of it.
   Mosca.   Is the lie   5
Safely conveyed amongst us? Is that sure?
Knows every man his burden?
   Corv.   Yes.
   Mosca.   Then shrink not.
   Corv. [*Aside to Mosca*] But knows the advocate the   10
   truth?
   Mosca. O sir,
By no means. I devised a formal tale
That salved your reputation. But be valiant, sir.
   Corv. I fear no one but him, that this his pleading   15
Should make him stand for a co-heir—
   Mosca.   Co-halter!
Hang him, we will but use his tongue, his noise,
As we do Croaker's here.
   Corv.   Ay, what shall he do?   20
   Mosca. When we ha' done, you mean?
   Corv.   Yes.
   Mosca.   Why, we'll think:
Sell him for mummia; he's half dust already.

(IV.ii.)
   1. CARRIAGE: meaning.
   7. BURDEN: responsibility.
   13. FORMAL: circumstantial.
   19. CROAKER'S: Corbaccio's.
   24. MUMMIA: mummy, a magic remedy made from preserved flesh.
   25. BUFFALO: horned one (cuckold).
   33. MERCURY: god of eloquence.
   34. FRENCH HERCULES: the eloquence of the Gallic Hercules was
symbolized by pictures showing him herding captives by chains from
his mouth to their ears.

(*To Voltore*) Do not you smile to see this buffalo,   25
How he doth sport it with his head? I should,
If all were well and past. (*To Corbaccio*) Sir, only you
Are he that shall enjoy the crop of all,
And these not know for whom they toil.

  Corb.   Ay, peace.   30

  Mosca. (*To Corvino*) But you shall eat it. [*Aside*]
    Much! (*To Voltore*) Worshipful sir,
Mercury sit upon your thund'ring tongue,
Or the French Hercules, and make your language
As conquering as his club, to beat along,   35
As with a tempest, flat, our adversaries;
But much more yours, sir.

  Volt.   Here they come; ha' done.

  Mosca. I have another witness, if you need, sir,
I can produce.   40

  Volt.   Who is it?

  Mosca.   Sir, I have her.

[*Enter Four Avocatori, Bonario, Celia, Notario,
       Commandadori, etc.*]

  1. Avo. The like of this the Senate never heard of.

  2. Avo. 'Twill come most strange to them, when
    we report it.   45

  4. Avo. The gentlewoman has been ever held
Of unreproved name.

  3. Avo.   So the young man.

  4. Avo. The more unnatural part that of his father.

  2. Avo. More of the husband.   50

  1. Avo.   I not know to give
His act a name, it is so monstrous!

  4. Avo. But the impostor, he is a thing created
T' exceed example!

  1. Avo.   And all aftertimes!   55

  2. Avo. I never heard a true voluptuary
Described but him.

3. Avo.   Appear yet those were cited?

Not. All but the old magnifico, Volpone.

1. Avo. Why is not he here?   60

Mosca.   Please your fatherhoods,
Here is his advocate. Himself's so weak,
So feeble—

4. Avo. What are you?

Bon.   His parasite,   65
His knave, his pander. I beseech the court
He may be forced to come, that your grave eyes
May bear strong witness of his strange impostures.

Volt. Upon my faith and credit with your virtues,
He is not able to endure the air.   70

2. Avo. Bring him, however.

3. Avo.   We will see him.

4. Avo. Fetch him.   [*Exeunt Officers.*]

Volt. Your fatherhoods' fit pleasures be obeyed,
But sure the sight will rather move your pities   75
Than indignation. May it please the court,
In the meantime he may be heard in me:
I know this place most void of prejudice,
And therefore crave it, since we have no reason
To fear our truth should hurt our cause.   80

3. Avo.   Speak free.

Volt. Then know, most honored fathers, I must now
Discover to your strangely abused ears
The most prodigious and most frontless piece
Of solid impudence and treachery   85
That ever vicious nature yet brought forth
To shame the state of Venice. This lewd woman,
That wants no artificial looks or tears

59. MAGNIFICO: wealthy magnate.
79. CRAVE: request.
83. ABUSED: deceived.
84. FRONTLESS: shameless.
90. CLOSE: secret.
94. TIMELESS: ill-timed; misplaced; BOUNTY: charity.
97. OWE: accept.
101. EXTIRP: destroy.
107. FACT: crime.
113. TURNS: turns of events.

To help the visor she has now put on,
Hath long been known a close adulteress   90
To that lascivious youth there; not suspected,
I say, but known, and taken in the act
With him; and by this man, the easy husband,
Pardoned; whose timeless bounty makes him now
Stand here, the most unhappy, innocent person   95
That ever man's own goodness made accused.
For these, not knowing how to owe a gift
Of that dear grace but with their shame; being placed
So above all powers of their gratitude,
Began to hate the benefit, and, in place   100
Of thanks, devise t' extirp the memory
Of such an act. Wherein I pray your fatherhoods
To observe the malice, yea, the rage, of creatures
Discovered in their evils, and what heart
Such take, even from their crimes. But that anon   105
Will more appear. This gentleman, the father,
Hearing of this foul fact, with many others,
Which daily struck at his too tender ears,
And grieved in nothing more than that he could not
Preserve himself a parent—his son's ills   110
Growing to that strange flood—at last decreed
To disinherit him.
    1. Avo. These be strange turns!
    2. Avo. The young man's fame was ever fair and
        honest.   115
    Volt. So much more full of danger is his vice,
That can beguile so under shade of virtue.
But, as I said, my honored sires, his father
Having this settled purpose—by what means
To him betrayed we know not—and this day   120
Appointed for the deed; that parricide,
I cannot style him better, by confederacy
Preparing this his paramour to be there,
Entered Volpone's house—who was the man,
Your fatherhoods must understand, designed   125

For the inheritance—there sought his father.
But with what purpose sought he him, my lords?
I tremble to pronounce it, that a son
Unto a father, and to such a father,
Should have so foul, felonious intent: 130
It was to murder him! When being prevented
By his more happy absence, what then did he?
Not check his wicked thoughts; no, now new deeds—
Mischief doth ever end where it begins—
An act of horror, fathers! He dragged forth   135
The aged gentleman that had there lain bedrid
Three years and more, out off his innocent couch,
Naked, upon the floor, there left him; wounded
His servant in the face; and with this strumpet,
The stale to his forged practice, who was glad   140
To be so active—I shall here desire
Your fatherhoods to note but my collections
As most remarkable—thought at once to stop
His father's ends, discredit his free choice
In the old gentleman, redeem themselves   145
By laying infamy upon this man,
To whom, with blushing, they should owe their lives.

    1. Avo. What proofs have you of this?
    Bon.   Most honored fathers,
I humbly crave there be no credit given   150
To this man's mercenary tongue.

    2. Avo.   Forbear.
    Bon. His soul moves in his fee.
    3. Avo.   O, sir!
    Bon.   This fellow   155
For six sols more would plead against his Maker.
    1. Avo. You do forget yourself.

---

140. STALE: decoy.
142. COLLECTIONS: evidence.
156. SOLS: French coins.
163. CREATURE: human being.
175. MERE PORTENT: perfect monster.
177. MADE: manipulated.
193. PARTRIDGE: harlot.

Volt.   Nay, nay, grave fathers,
Let him have scope. Can any man imagine
That he will spare 's accuser that would not   160
Have spared his parent?
    1. Avo.   Well, produce your proofs.
    Celia. I would I could forget I were a creature!
    Volt. Signor Corbaccio!
    4. Avo.   What is he?   165
    Volt.   The father.
    2. Avo. Has he had an oath?
    Not.   Yes.
    Corb.   What must I do now?
    Not. Your testimony's craved.   170
    Corb.   Speak to the knave?
I'll ha' my mouth first stopped with earth. My heart
Abhors his knowledge. I disclaim in him.
    1. Avo. But for what cause?
    Corb.   The mere portent of nature.   175
He is an utter stranger to my loins.
    Bon. Have they made you to this?
    Corb.   I will not hear thee,
Monster of men, swine, goat, wolf, parricide!
Speak not, thou viper.   180
    Bon.   Sir, I will sit down
And rather wish my innocence should suffer
Than I resist the authority of a father.
    Volt. Signor Corvino!
    2. Avo.   This is strange.   185
    1. Avo.   Who's this?
    Not. The husband.
    4. Avo.   Is he sworn?
    Not.   He is.
    3. Avo.   Speak, then.   190
    Corv. This woman, please your fatherhoods, is a
        whore
Of most hot exercise, more than a partridge,
Upon record—

1. Avo. No more.   195
Corv.   Neighs like a jennet.
Not. Preserve the honor of the court.
Corv.   I shall,
And modesty of your most reverend ears.
And yet I hope that I may say these eyes   200
Have seen her glued unto that piece of cedar,
That fine, well-timbered gallant; and that here
The letters may be read, thorough the horn,
That make the story perfect.
Mosca. [Aside]   Excellent, sir!   205
Corv. [Aside] There is no shame in this now, is
    there?
Mosca. [Aside]   None.
Corv. Or if I said I hoped that she were onward
To her damnation, if there be a hell   210
Greater than whore and woman; a good Catholic
May make the doubt.
3. Avo.   His grief hath made him frantic.
1. Avo. Remove him hence.   *[Celia] swoons.*
2. Avo.   Look to the woman.   215
Corv.   Rare!
Prettily feigned again!
4. Avo.   Stand from about her.
1. Avo. Give her the air.
3. Avo. [To Mosca]   What can you say?   220
Mosca.   My wound,
May 't please your wisdoms, speaks for me, received
In aid of my good patron when he missed
His sought-for father, when that well-taught dame
Had her cue given her to cry out a rape.   225

---

196. JENNET: Spanish horse.
203. THOROUGH: through; HORN: referring to the cuckold's horns
(symbolized by the letter "V") and the sheeting of horn over the
alphabet on a hornbook.
226. LAID: premeditated.
252. HYENA: reputed to shed hypocritical tears over its victims.
257. EXORBITANT: out of bounds.

Bon. O most laid impudence! Fathers—
3. *Avo.*   Sir, be silent;
You had your hearing free, so must they theirs.
 2. *Avo.* I do begin to doubt the imposture here.
 4. *Avo.* This woman has too many moods.   230
Volt.   Grave fathers,
She is a creature of a most professed
And prostituted lewdness.
 Corv.   Most impetuous,
Unsatisfied, grave fathers!   235
Volt.   May her feignings
Not take your wisdoms; but this day she baited
A stranger, a grave knight, with her loose eyes
And more lascivious kisses. This man saw 'em
Together on the water in a gondola.   240
Mosca. Here is the lady herself, that saw 'em too,
Without; who then had in the open streets
Pursued them, but for saving her knight's honor.
 1. *Avo.* Produce that lady.
 2. *Avo.*   Let her come. [*Exit Mosca.*] 245
 4. *Avo.*   These things,
They strike with wonder!
 3. *Avo.*   I am turned a stone!

[*Re-enter Mosca with Lady Wouldbe.*]

Mosca. Be resolute, madam.
Lady.   Ay, this same is she.   250
Out, thou chameleon harlot! Now thine eyes
Vie tears with the hyena. Darest thou look
Upon my wronged face? I cry your pardons.
I fear I have forgettingly transgressed
Against the dignity of the court—   255
 2. *Avo.*   No, madam,
Lady. And been exorbitant—
 4. *Avo.*   You have not, lady,
These proofs are strong.

Lady.   Surely, I had no purpose   260
To scandalize your honors, or my sex's.

   3. *Avo*. We do believe it.

   Lady.   Surely you may believe it.

   2. *Avo*. Madam, we do.

   Lady.   Indeed you may, my breeding   265
Is not so coarse—

   4. *Avo*.   We know it.

   Lady.   To offend
With pertinacy—

   3. *Avo*.   Lady—   270

   Lady.   Such a presence!
No surely.

   1. *Avo*. We well think it.

   Lady.   You may think it.

   1. *Avo*. Let her o'ercome. What witnesses have you,   275
To make good your report?

   Bon.   Our consciences.

   Celia. And heaven, that never fails the innocent.

   4. *Avo*. These are no testimonies.

   Bon.   Not in your courts,   280
Where multitude and clamor overcomes.

   1. *Avo*. Nay, then, you do wax insolent.

Volpone is brought in, as impotent.

   Volt.   Here, here
The testimony comes that will convince
And put to utter dumbness their bold tongues!   285
See here, grave fathers, here's the ravisher,
The rider on men's wives, the great impostor,
The grand voluptuary! Do you not think

---

269. PERTINACY: malicious persistence.
275. O'ERCOME: i.e., have the last word.
289. VENERY: lust.
297. STRAPPADO: torture instrument that dislocated the joints.
303. EQUAL: just.
316. FLESHED: encouraged (by past successes).
319. SEVER: separate.
320. PRODIGIES: monsters.

These limbs should affect venery? Or these eyes
Covet a concubine? Pray you mark these hands;   290
Are they not fit to stroke a lady's breasts?
Perhaps he doth dissemble?
 Bon.   So he does.
 Volt. Would you ha' him tortured?
 Bon.   I would have him proved. 295
 Volt. Best try him then with goads, or burning irons;
Put him to the strappado. I have heard
The rack hath cured the gout—faith, give it him,
And help him of a malady; be courteous.
I'll undertake, before these honored fathers,   300
He shall have yet as many left diseases
As she has known adulterers or thou strumpets.
O my most equal hearers, if these deeds,
Acts of this bold and most exorbitant strain,
May pass with sufferance, what one citizen   305
But owes the forfeit of his life, yea, fame,
To him that dares traduce him? Which of you
Are safe, my honored fathers? I would ask,
With leave of your grave fatherhoods, if their plot
Have any face or color like to truth?   310
Or if, unto the dullest nostril here,
It smell not rank and most abhorred slander?
I crave your care of this good gentleman,
Whose life is much endangered by their fable;
And as for them, I will conclude with this: 315
That vicious persons, when they are hot and fleshed
In impious acts, their constancy abounds.
Damned deeds are done with greatest confidence.
 1. Avo. Take 'em to custody, and sever them.
 2. Avo. 'Tis pity two such prodigies should live.   320
 1. Avo. Let the old gentleman be returned with care.
    [*Exeunt Officers with Volpone.*]
I'm sorry our credulity wronged him.
 4. Avo. These are two creatures!

   3. Avo.   I have an earthquake in me!

   2. Avo. Their shame, even in their cradles, fled their   325
faces.

   4. Avo. [*To Voltore*] You've done a worthy service
to the state, sir,

In their discovery.

   1. Avo.   You shall hear ere night   330

What punishment the court decrees upon 'em.

     [*Exeunt Avocatori, Notario, and Commandadori
                with Bonario and Celia.*]

   Volt. We thank your fatherhoods. How like you it?

   Mosca.   Rare.

I'd ha' your tongue, sir, tipped with gold for this;

I'd ha' you be the heir to the whole city;   335

The earth I'ld have want men ere you want living.

They're bound to erect your statue in St. Mark's.

Signor Corvino, I would have you go

And show yourself, that you have conquered.

   Corv.   Yes.   340

   Mosca. It was much better that you should profess
Yourself a cuckold thus, than that the other

Should have been proved.

   Corv.   Nay, I considered that.

Now it is her fault.   345

   Mosca.   Then it had been yours.

   Corv. True. I do doubt this advocate still.

   Mosca.   I' faith,

You need not; I dare ease you of that care.

   Corv. I trust thee, Mosca.   [*Exit.*]   350

   Mosca.   As your own soul, sir.

   Corb.   Mosca!

   Mosca. Now for your business, sir.

   Corb.   How! Ha' you business?

   Mosca. Yes, yours, sir.   355

---

336. WANT: lack.
359. REST . . . EYES: i.e., don't worry.

Corb.   O, none else?

Mosca.   None else, not I.

Corb. Be careful, then.

Mosca.   Rest you with both your eyes, sir.

Corb. Dispatch it.   360

Mosca.   Instantly.

Corb.   And look that all
Whatever be put in, jewels, plate, moneys,
Household stuff, bedding, curtains.

Mosca.   Curtain-rings, sir;   365
Only the advocate's fee must be deducted.

Corb. I'll pay him now; you'll be too prodigal.

Mosca. Sir, I must tender it.

Corb.   Two *cecchines* is well?

Mosca. No, six, sir.   370

Corb.   'Tis too much.

Mosca.   He talked a great while,
You must consider that, sir.

Corb.   Well, there's three—

Mosca. I'll give it him.   375

Corb.   Do so, and there's for thee.
                                                    [*Exit.*]

Mosca. [*Aside*] Bountiful bones! What horrid
    strange offense
Did he commit 'gainst nature, in his youth,
Worthy this age? [*To Voltore*] You see, sir, how I   380
    work
Unto your ends; take you no notice.

Volt.   No,
I'll leave you.   [*Exit.*]

Mosca.   All is yours, the Devil and all,   385
Good advocate! Madam, I'll bring you home.

Lady. No, I'll go see your patron.

Mosca.   That you shall not.
I'll tell you why: my purpose is to urge
My patron to reform his will, and for   390

The zeal you've shown today, whereas before
You were but third or fourth, you shall be now
Put in the first; which would appear as begged
If you were present. Therefore—
    Lady. You shall sway me.　　　　　　　　　395

                  [*Exeunt.*]

(V.i.)
1. BRUNT: crisis.
4. CAVE: beware.

ACT V

Scene I

[Enter Volpone.]

Volp. Well, I am here, and all this brunt is past.
I ne'er was in dislike with my disguise
Till this fled moment. Here 'twas good, in private;
But in your public—*Cave,* whilst I breathe.
'Fore God, my left leg 'gan to have the cramp,   5
And I apprehended straight some power had struck me
With a dead palsy. Well, I must be merry
And shake it off. A many of these fears
Would put me into some villainous disease,
Should they come thick upon me. I'll prevent 'em.   10
Give me a bowl of lusty wine, to fright
This humor from my heart. (*Drinks.*) Hum, hum, hum!
'Tis almost gone already; I shall conquer.
Any device, now, of rare, ingenious knavery,
That would possess me with a violent laughter,   15
Would make me up again. (*Drinks again.*) So, so, so,
    so!
This heat is life; 'tis blood by this time! Mosca!

[Enter Mosca.]

Mosca. How now, sir? Does the day look clear
    again?   20
Are we recovered and wrought out of error
Into our way, to see our path before us?
Is our trade free once more?
    Volp.   Exquisite Mosca!
    Mosca. Was it not carried learnedly?   25

Volp.   And stoutly.
Good wits are greatest in extremities.
    Mosca. It were a folly beyond thought to trust
Any grand act unto a cowardly spirit.
You are not taken with it enough, methinks.   30
    Volp. O, more than if I had enjoyed the wench.
The pleasure of all womankind's not like it.
    Mosca. Why, now you speak, sir. We must here be
        fixed;
Here we must rest. This is our masterpiece;   35
We cannot think to go beyond this.
    Volp.   True,
Th'ast played thy prize, my precious Mosca.
    Mosca.   Nay, sir,
To gull the court—   40
    Volp.   And quite divert the torrent
Upon the innocent.
    Mosca.   Yes, and to make
So rare a music out of discords—
    Volp.   Right.   45
That yet to me's the strangest; how th'ast borne it!
That these, being so divided 'mongst themselves,
Should not scent somewhat, or in me or thee,
Or doubt their own side.
    Mosca.   True, they will not see't.   50
Too much light blinds 'em, I think. Each of 'em
Is so possessed and stuffed with his own hopes
That anything unto the contrary,
Never so true, or never so apparent,
Never so palpable, they will resist it—   55
    Volp. Like a temptation of the Devil.
    Mosca.   Right, sir.
Merchants may talk of trade, and your great signors

---

60. GLEBE: cultivable land.
81. COZENED: cheated.
85. DRAW . . . HEADS: arrange the matter by subjects; AGGRAVATE:
exaggerate.
87. SHIFT . . . SHIRT: disarrange his clothing in violent gesticulation.
90. ANSWER: repay.

Of land that yields well; but if Italy
Have any glebe more fruitful than these fellows,   60
I am deceived. Did not your advocate rare?
   Volp. O—"My most honored fathers, my grave fa-
     thers,
Under correction of your fatherhoods,
What face of truth is here? If these strange deeds   65
May pass, most honored fathers"—I had much ado
To forbear laughing.
   Mosca.   'T seemed to me you sweat, sir.
   Volp. In troth, I did a little.
   Mosca.   But confess, sir,   70
Were you not daunted?
   Volp.   In good faith, I was
A little in a mist, but not dejected;
Never, but still myself.
   Mosca.   I think it, sir.   75
Now, so truth help me, I must needs say this, sir,
And out of conscience for your advocate:
He's taken pains, in faith, sir, and deserved,
In my poor judgment—I speak it under favor,
Not to contrary you, sir—very richly—   80
Well—to be cozened.
   Volp.   Troth, and I think so too,
By that I heard him in the latter end.
   Mosca. O, but before, sir, had you heard him first
Draw it to certain heads, then aggravate,   85
Then use his vehement figures—I looked still
When he would shift a shirt; and doing this
Out of pure love, no hope of gain—
   Volp.   'Tis right.
I cannot answer him, Mosca, as I would,   90
Not yet; but for thy sake, at thy entreaty,
I will begin ev'n now—to vex 'em all,
This very instant.
   Mosca.   Good, sir.

Volp.   Call the dwarf   95
And eunuch forth.
  Mosca.   Castrone! Nano!

[*Enter Castrone and Nano.*]

  Nano.   Here.
  Volp. Shall we have a jig now?
  Mosca.   What you please, sir.   100
  Volp.   Go,
Straight give out about the streets, you two,
That I am dead; do it with constancy,
Sadly, do you hear? Impute it to the grief
Of this late slander.   [*Exeunt Castrone and Nano.*]   105
  Mosca.   What do you mean, sir?
  Volp.   O,
I shall have instantly my vulture, crow,
Raven, come flying hither on the news,
To peck for carrion, my she-wolf and all,   110
Greedy and full of expectation—
  Mosca. And then to have it ravished from their
    mouths?
  Volp. 'Tis true. I will ha' thee put on a gown,
And take upon thee as thou wert mine heir;   115
Show 'em a will. Open that chest and reach
Forth one of those that has the blanks. I'll straight
Put in thy name.
  Mosca.   It will be rare, sir.
  Volp.   Ay,   120
When they e'en gape, and find themselves deluded—
  Mosca. Yes.

---

99. JIG: farce.
103. CONSTANCY: fidelity; i.e., convincingly.
142. CLARISSIMO: grandee (Corbaccio).
143. CRUMP YOU: curl up before you.
157. GIRDLE: the *cestus* of Venus, which contained her magic allure.
159. ACRISIUS: father of Danaë, who was visited by Jove in a shower of gold despite all of her father's precautions.

Volp.   And thou use them scurvily! Dispatch,
Get on thy gown.

    Mosca.   But what, sir, if they ask   125
After the body?

    Volp.   Say it was corrupted.

    Mosca. I'll say it stunk, sir; and was fain t' have it
Coffined up instantly and sent away.

    Volp. Anything; what thou wilt. Hold, here's my 130
    will.
Get thee a cap, a count-book, pen and ink,
Papers afore thee; sit as thou wert taking
An inventory of parcels. I'll get up
Behind the curtain, on a stool, and hearken;   135
Sometime peep over, see how they do look,
With what degrees their blood doth leave their
    faces.
O, 'twill afford me a rare meal of laughter!

    Mosca. Your advocate will turn stark dull upon it. 140

    Volp. It will take off his oratory's edge.

    Mosca. But your *clarissimo*, old round-back, he
Will crump you like a hog louse with the touch.

    Volp. And what Corvino?

    Mosca.   O sir, look for him   145
Tomorrow morning, with a rope and dagger,
To visit all the streets; he must run mad.
My lady too, that came into the court
To bear false witness for your Worship—

    Volp.   Yes,   150
And kissed me 'fore the fathers, when my face
Flowed all with oils—

    Mosca.   And sweat, sir. Why, your gold
Is such another med'cine, it dries up
All those offensive savors! It transforms   155
The most deformed and restores 'em lovely
As 'twere the strange poetical girdle. Jove
Could not invent t' himself a shroud more subtle
To pass Acrisius' guards. It is the thing

Makes all the world her grace, her youth, her beauty. 160
  Volp. I think she loves me.
  Mosca.   Who? The lady, sir?
She's jealous of you.
  Volp.   Dost thou say so?
                       [*Knocking heard.*]
  Mosca.   Hark,   165
There's some already.
  Volp.   Look.
  Mosca.   It is the vulture;
He has the quickest scent.
  Volp.   I'll to my place,   170
Thou to thy posture.
  Mosca.   I am set.
  Volp.   But, Mosca,
Play the artificer, now, torture 'em rarely.

[*Enter Voltore.*]

  Volt. How now, my Mosca?   175
  Mosca. [*Writing*]   "Turkey carpets, nine—"
  Volt. Taking an inventory? That is well.
  Mosca. "Two suits of bedding, tissue—"
  Volt.   Where's the will?
Let me read that the while.   180

[*Enter Servitori with Corbaccio in a chair.*]

  Corb.   So, set me down,
And get you home.   [*Exeunt Servitori.*]
  Volt. Is he come now, to trouble us?
  Mosca. "Of cloth of gold, two more—"
  Corb.   Is it done, Mosca?   185

---

171. POSTURE: role.
174. ARTIFICER: craftsman.
178. SUITS: sets; TISSUE: a rich fabric.
S.D. 190. TRAVERSE: curtain.
196. IS . . . SPUN: is he dead?
202. DIAPER: linen napery.
213. GARTERS: reference to the proverbial saying to "hang oneself in one's own garters."

Mosca. "Of several velvets, eight—"
Volt.   I like his care.
Corb. Dost thou not hear?

[*Enter Corvino.*]

Corv.   Ha! Is the hour come, Mosca?
Volp. (*Peeps from behind a traverse*) Ay, now they   190
  muster.
Corv.   What does the advocate here,
Or this Corbaccio?
Corb.   What do these here?

[*Enter Lady Wouldbe.*]

Lady.   Mosca!   195
Is his thread spun?
Mosca.   "Eight chests of linen—"
Volp.   O,
My fine Dame Wouldbe, too!
Corv.   Mosca, the will,   200
That I may show it these and rid 'em hence.
Mosca. "Six chests of diaper, four of damask—"
    There.   [*Gives them the will.*]
Corb. Is that the will?
Mosca.   "Down beds and bolsters—"   205
Volp.   Rare!
Be busy still. Now they begin to flutter;
They never think of me. Look, see, see, see!
How their swift eyes run over the long deed,
Unto the name and to the legacies,   210
What is bequeathed them there—
Mosca.   "Ten suits of hangings—"
Volp. Ay, i' their garters, Mosca. Now their hopes
Are at the gasp.
Volt.   Mosca the heir!   215
Corb.   What's that?

Volp. My advocate is dumb; look to my merchant,
He has heard of some strange storm, a ship is lost,
He faints; my lady will swoon. Old glazen-eyes
He hath not reached his despair yet.   220
     Corb.   All these
Are out of hope; I'm sure the man.
     Corv.   But, Mosca—
     Mosca. "Two cabinets—"
     Corv.   Is this in earnest?   225
     Mosca.   "One
Of ebony—"
     Corv.   Or do you but delude me?
     Mosca. "The other, mother-of-pearl"—I am very busy.
Good faith, it is a fortune thrown upon me—   230
"Item, one salt of agate"—not my seeking.
     Lady. Do you hear, sir?
     Mosca.   "A perfumed box"—Pray you forbear,
You see I'm troubled—"made of an onyx—"
     Lady.   How!   235
     Mosca. Tomorrow or next day I shall be at leisure
To talk with you all.
     Corv.   Is this my large hope's issue?
     Lady. Sir, I must have a fairer answer.
     Mosca.   Madam!   240
Marry, and shall: pray you, fairly quit my house.
Nay, raise no tempest with your looks; but hark you,
Remember what your Ladyship offered me
To put you in, an heir; go to, think on 't;
And what you said e'en your best madams did   245
For maintenance, and why not you? Enough.
Go home, and use the poor Sir Poll, your knight, well,
For fear I tell some riddles. Go, be melancholic.
                              [*Exit Lady Wouldbe.*]

231. SALT: saltcellar.
238. ISSUE: outcome.
257. WITTOL: contented cuckold.
270. FOUR EYES: eyes with the aid of spectacles.
272. HARLOT: base knave.
276. THREE LEGS: supported by a cane.

Volp. O my fine devil!

Corv.   Mosca, pray you a word.   250

Mosca. Lord! Will not you take your dispatch hence
    yet?

Methinks of all you should have been the example.

Why should you stay here? With what thought? What
    promise?   255

Hear you, do not you know I know you an ass,

And that you would most fain have been a wittol,

If fortune would have let you? That you are

A declared cuckold, on good terms? This pearl,

You'll say, was yours? Right. This diamond?   260

I'll not deny't, but thank you. Much here else?

It may be so. Why, think that these good works

May help to hide your bad. I'll not betray you;

Although you be but extraordinary,

And have it only in title, it sufficeth.   265

Go home, be melancholic too, or mad. [*Exit Corvino.*]

Volp. Rare, Mosca! How his villainy becomes him!

Volt. Certain, he doth delude all these for me.

Corb. Mosca the heir?

Volp.   O, his four eyes have found it!   270

Corb. I'm cozened, cheated, by a parasite slave!

Harlot, th'ast gulled me.

Mosca.   Yes, sir. Stop your mouth,

Or I shall draw the only tooth is left.

Are not you he, that filthy, covetous wretch   275

With the three legs, that here, in hope of prey,

Have, any time this three year, snuffed about

With your most grov'ling nose; and would have hired

Me to the pois'ning of my patron, sir?

Are not you he that have today in court   280

Professed the disinheriting of your son?

Perjured yourself? Go home, and die, and stink;

If you but croak a syllable, all comes out.

Away, and call your porters!   [*Exit Corbaccio.*]

    Go, go, stink.   285

Volp. Excellent varlet!

Volt.   Now, my faithful Mosca,
I find thy constancy—

Mosca.   Sir?

Volt.   Sincere.   290

Mosca.   "A table
Of porphyry"—I mar'l you'll be thus troublesome.

Volt. Nay, leave off now, they are gone.

Mosca.   Why, who are you?
What! Who did send for you? O, cry you mercy,   295
Reverend sir! Good faith, I am grieved for you,
That any chance of mine should thus defeat
Your—I must needs say—most deserving travails.
But I protest, sir, it was cast upon me,
And I could almost wish to be without it,   300
But that the will o' the dead must be observed.
Marry, my joy is that you need it not;
You have a gift, sir—thank your education—
Will never let you want while there are men
And malice to breed causes. Would I had   305
But half the like, for all my fortune, sir.
If I have any suits—as I do hope,
Things being so easy and direct, I shall not—
I will make bold with your obstreperous aid,
Conceive me, for your fee, sir. In meantime,   310
You that have so much law I know ha' the conscience
Not to be covetous of what is mine.
Good sir, I thank you for my plate; 'twill help
To set up a young man. Good faith, you look
As you were costive; best go home and purge, sir.   315
                              [*Exit Voltore.*]

---

292. MAR'L: marvel.
297. CHANCE: fortune.
305. CAUSES: lawsuits.
315. COSTIVE: constipated
316. LETTUCE: a laxative.
319. HABIT: clothing.
338. THE . . . CURST: proverbial saying.

(V.ii.)
5. ZANT: Zante, an island off Greece.

Volp. Bid him eat lettuce well. My witty mischief,
Let me embrace thee. O that I could now
Transform thee to a Venus—Mosca, go,
Straight take my habit of *clarissimo*,
And walk the streets; be seen, torment 'em more.   320
We must pursue as well as plot. Who would
Have lost this feast?
   Mosca.   I doubt it will lose them.
   Volp. O, my recovery shall recover all.
That I could now but think on some disguise   325
To meet 'em in and ask 'em questions;
How I would vex 'em still at every turn!
   Mosca. Sir, I can fit you.
   Volp.   Canst thou?
   Mosca.   Yes, I know   330
One o' the *commandadori*, sir, so like you,
Him will I straight make drunk, and bring you his
    habit.
   Volp. A rare disguise, and answering thy brain!
O, I will be a sharp disease unto 'em.   335
   Mosca. Sir, you must look for curses—
   Volp.   Till they burst;
The fox fares ever best when he is curst.
                           [*Exeunt.*]

Scene [II]

[*Enter Peregrine, disguised, and Three Mercatori.*]

   Per. Am I enough disguised?
   1. Mer.   I warrant you.
   Per. All my ambition is to fright him only.
   2. Mer. If you could ship him away, 'twere excellent.
   3. Mer. To Zant, or to Aleppo!   5
   Per.   Yes, and ha' his

Adventures put i' the book of voyages,
And his gulled story registered for truth.
Well, gentlemen, when I am in a while,
And that you think us warm in our discourse,   10
Know your approaches.
  1. Mer.   Trust it to our care.
          [*Exeunt Mercatori.*]

     [*Enter Woman.*]

 Per. Save you, fair lady! Is Sir Poll within?
 Wom. I do not know, sir.
 Per.   Pray you say unto him   15
Here is a merchant, upon earnest business,
Desires to speak with him.
 Wom.   I will see, sir.   [*Exit.*]
 Per.   Pray you.
I see the family is all female here.   20

    [*Re-enter Woman.*]

 Wom. He says, sir, he has weighty affairs of state
That now require him whole; some other time
You may possess him.
 Per.   Pray you say again,
If those require him whole, these will exact him,   25
Whereof I bring him tidings. [*Exit Woman.*] What
  might be
His grave affair of state now? How to make
Bolognian sausages here in Venice, sparing
One o' the ingredients?   30

---

 7. BOOK . . . VOYAGES: such as Richard Hakluyt's collections of travel narratives.
 8. GULLED STORY: story of how he was duped.
 22. HIM WHOLE: his full attention.
 25. EXACT: demand.
 32. NO STATESMAN: because a statesman would have said "intelligence."
 47. PUNK: prostitute.

[*Re-enter Woman.*]

  Wom.   Sir, he says he knows
By your word "tidings" that you are no statesman,
And therefore wills you stay.
  Per.   Sweet, pray you return him,
I have not read so many proclamations   35
And studied them for words as he has done,
But—Here he deigns to come.   [*Exit Woman.*]

[*Enter Sir Politic.*]

  Sir Pol.   Sir, I must crave
Your courteous pardon. There hath chanced today
Unkind disaster 'twixt my lady and me,   40
And I was penning my apology
To give her satisfaction as you came now.
  Per. Sir, I am grieved I bring you worse disaster:
The gentleman you met at the port today,
That told you he was newly arrived—   45
  Sir Pol.   Ay, was
A fugitive punk?
  Per.   No, sir, a spy set on you;
And he has made relation to the Senate
That you professed to him to have a plot   50
To sell the state of Venice to the Turk.
  Sir Pol. O me!
  Per.   For which warrants are signed by this
    time,
To apprehend you and to search your study   55
For papers—
  Sir Pol.   Alas, sir, I have none but notes
Drawn out of playbooks—
  Per.   All the better, sir.
  Sir Pol. And some essays. What shall I do?   60
  Per.   Sir, best
Convey yourself into a sugar-chest,

Or, if you could lie round, a frail were rare;
And I could send you aboard.
    Sir Pol.   Sir, I but talked so   65
For discourse sake merely.   *They knock without.*
    Per.   Hark! They are there.
    Sir Pol. I am a wretch, a wretch!
    Per.   What will you do, sir?
Ha' you ne'er a currant-butt to leap into?   70
They'll put you to the rack; you must be sudden.
    Sir Pol. Sir, I have an engine—
    3. Mer. [*Within*]   Sir Politic Wouldbe!
    2. Mer. [*Within*] Where is he?
    Sir Pol.   That I have thought upon beforetime.   75
    Per. What is it?
    Sir Pol.   I shall ne'er endure the torture!
Marry, it is, sir, of a tortoise shell,
Fitted for these extremities. Pray you, sir, help me.
Here I've a place, sir, to put back my legs;   80
Please you to lay it on, sir. With this cap
And my black gloves, I'll lie, sir, like a tortoise,
Till they are gone.
    Per.   And call you this an engine?
    Sir Pol. Mine own device. Good sir, bid my wife's   85
    women
To burn my papers.

          The Three Mercatori rush in.

    1. Mer.   Where's he hid?
    3. Mer.   We must,
And will sure, find him.   90
    2. Mer.   Which is his study?

---

63. FRAIL: basket.
70. CURRANT-BUTT: barrel for currants.
72. ENGINE: device.
126. MOTION: spectacle.
128. TERM: session of the law courts.

1. Mer.   What
Are you, sir?
  Per.   I'm a merchant, that came here
To look upon this tortoise.   95
  3. Mer.   How!
  1. Mer.   St. Mark!
What beast is this?
  Per.   It is a fish.
  2. Mer.   Come out here!   100
  Per. Nay, you may strike him, sir, and tread upon
      him.
He'll bear a cart.
  1. Mer. What, to run over him?
  Per.   Yes.   105
  3. Mer. Let's jump upon him.
  2. Mer.   Can he not go?
  Per.   He creeps, sir.
  1. Mer. Let's see him creep.
  Per.   No, good sir, you will hurt him. 110
  2. Mer. Heart, I'll see him creep or prick his guts!
  3. Mer. Come out here!
  Per.   Pray you, sir. [*Aside to Sir Politic.*]
Creep a little.
  1. Mer.   Forth.   115
  2. Mer.   Yet further.
  Per.   Good sir!—Creep.
  2. Mer.   We'll see his legs.
          They pull off the shell and discover him.
  3. Mer. God's so', he has garters!
  1. Mer.   Ay, and gloves!   120
  2. Mer.   Is this
Your fearful tortoise?
  Per.   Now, Sir Poll, we are even;
For your next project I shall be prepared.
I am sorry for the funeral of your notes, sir.   125
  1. Mer. 'Twere a rare motion to be seen in Fleet
      Street.

2. Mer. Ay, i' the term.
1. Mer.   Or Smithfield, in the fair.
3. Mer. Methinks 'tis but a melancholic sight.   130
Per. Farewell, most politic tortoise!
              [*Exeunt Peregrine and Mercatori.*]

[*Re-enter Woman.*]

Sir Pol.   Where's my lady?
Knows she of this?
Wom.   I know not, sir.
Sir Pol.   Inquire.   135
              [*Exit Woman.*]
O, I shall be the fable of all feasts,
The freight of the *gazetti*, shipboys' tale,
And, which is worst, even talk for ordinaries.

[*Re-enter Woman.*]

Wom. My lady's come most melancholic home,
And says, sir, she will straight to sea, for physic.   140
Sir Pol. And I, to shun this place and clime forever,
Creeping with house on back, and think it well
To shrink my poor head in my politic shell.
              [*Exeunt.*]

137. FREIGHT: subject matter; GAZETTI: tabloids.
138. ORDINARIES: taverns.

(V.iii.)
3. SEVER: tell apart.
14. ON: of.
15. CASE: garments.
16. COMPOSITION: agreement.

\

Scene [III]

*[Enter Volpone in the habit of a commandadore, and
           Mosca in that of a clarissimo.]*

Volp. Am I then like him?
Mosca.   O sir, you are he;
No man can sever you.
  Volp.   Good.
  Mosca.   But what am I?   5
  Volp. 'Fore heav'n, a brave *clarissimo*, thou be-
     comest it!
Pity thou wert not born one.
  Mosca. [*Aside*]   If I hold
My made one, 'twill be well.   10
  Volp.   I'll go and see
What news first at the court.   [*Exit.*]
  Mosca.   Do so. My fox
Is out on his hole, and ere he shall re-enter,
I'll make him languish in his borrowed case,   15
Except he come to composition with me.
Androgyno, Castrone, Nano!

[Enter Androgyno, Castrone, and Nano.]

All.   Here.
  Mosca. Go recreate yourselves abroad; go sport.
                                     [*Exeunt.*]
So, now I have the keys and am possessed.   20
Since he will needs be dead afore his time,
I'll bury him or gain by him. I'm his heir,
And so will keep me till he share at least.
To cozen him of all were but a cheat
Well placed; no man would construe it a sin.   25
Let his sport pay for 't. This is called the fox-trap.
                                     [*Exit.*]

Scene [IV]

[*Enter Corbaccio and Corvino.*]

Corb. They say the court is set.

Corv.   We must maintain
Our first tale good, for both our reputations.

Corb. Why, mine's no tale! My son would there
   have killed me.   5

Corv. That's true, I had forgot. [*Aside*] Mine is, I'm
   sure.—
But for your will, sir.

Corb.   Ay, I'll come upon him
For that hereafter, now his patron's dead.   10

[*Enter Volpone.*]

Volp. Signor Corvino! And Corbaccio! Sir,
Much joy unto you.

Corv.   Of what?

Volp.   The sudden good
Dropped down upon you—   15

Corb.   Where?

Volp.   And none knows how,
From old Volpone, sir.

Corb.   Out, arrant knave!

Volp. Let not your too much wealth, sir, make you 20
   furious.

Corb. Away, thou varlet.

Volp.   Why, sir?

Corb.   Dost thou mock me?

(V.iv.)
19. ARRANT: absolute.
28. BELIKE: perhaps.
34. AVOID: begone.
41. A'KNOWN: recognized.
55. OUT . . . REPARATIONS: in disrepair.
57. PISCARIA: fish market.

Volp. You mock the world, sir; did you not change   25
   wills?
Corb. Out, harlot!
Volp.   O! Belike you are the man,
Signor Corvino? Faith, you carry it well;
You grow not mad withal. I love your spirit.   30
You are not overleavened with your fortune.
You should ha' some would swell now, like a winevat,
With such an autumn—Did he gi' you all, sir?
  Corv. Avoid, you rascal.
Volp.   Troth, your wife has shown   35
Herself a very woman! But you are well,
You need not care; you have a good estate
To bear it out, sir, better by this chance—
Except Corbaccio have a share.
  Corb.   Hence, varlet.   40
  Volp. You will not be a'known, sir? Why, 'tis wise.
Thus do all gamesters, at all games, dissemble.
No man will seem to win.
             [*Exeunt Corvino and Corbaccio.*]
    Here comes my vulture,
Heaving his beak up i' the air and snuffing.   45

        [*Enter Voltore.*]

  Volt. Outstripped thus by a parasite? a slave,
Would run on errands and make legs for crumbs!
Well, what I'll do—
  Volp.   The court stays for your Worship.
I e'en rejoice, sir, at your Worship's happiness,   50
And that it fell into so learned hands,
That understand the fingering—
  Volt.   What do you mean?
  Volp. I mean to be a suitor to your Worship,
For the small tenement, out of reparations,   55
That at the end of your long row of houses,
By the *piscaria*—it was, in Volpone's time,

Your predecessor, ere he grew diseased,
A handsome, pretty, customed bawdyhouse
As any was in Venice, none dispraised;   60
But fell with him. His body and that house
Decayed together.
    Volt.   Come, sir, leave your prating.
    Volp. Why, if your Worship give me but your hand,
That I may ha' the refusal, I have done.   65
'Tis a mere toy to you, sir, candlerents.
As your learned Worship knows—
    Volt.   What do I know?
    Volp. Marry, no end of your wealth, sir, God de-
      crease it!   70
    Volt. Mistaking knave! What, mockst thou my mis-
      fortune?   [*Exit.*]
    Volp. His blessing on your heart, sir; would 'twere
      more!
Now to my first again, at the next corner.   75
                              [*Exit.*]

Scene [V]

[*Enter Corbaccio and Corvino. Mosca passes by
them.*]

    Corb. See, in our habit! See the impudent varlet!
    Corv. That I could shoot mine eyes at him, like gun-
      stones!

---

59. CUSTOMED: busy.
66. CANDLERENTS: rents from property constantly depreciating in value.

(V.v.)
2-3. GUNSTONES: cannon balls made of stone.
8. OVERREACHED: outdone; hoodwinked; BROOKED: could tolerate.
11. BANE: destruction.
16. MORAL EMBLEMS: allegorical designs with moral mottoes (with specific reference to the fable of Aesop).
22. JOLTHEAD: blockhead; CECCHINES: sequin buttons.
23. WARRANT: license.

[*Enter Volpone.*]

Volp. But is this true, sir, of the parasite?

Corb. Again t' afflict us? Monster!   5

Volp.   In good faith, sir,
I'm heartily grieved a beard of your grave length
Should be so overreached. I never brooked
That parasite's hair; methought his nose should cozen.
There still was somewhat in his look did promise   10
The bane of a *clarissimo.*

Corb.   Knave—

Volp.   Methinks
Yet you, that are so traded i' the world,
A witty merchant, the fine bird, Corvino,   15
That have such moral emblems on your name,
Should not have sung your shame and dropped your
     cheese
To let the fox laugh at your emptiness.

Corv. Sirrah, you think the privilege of the place   20
And your red saucy cap, that seems to me
Nailed to your jolthead with those two *cecchines,*
Can warrant your abuses. Come you hither.
You shall perceive, sir, I dare beat you. Approach.

Volp. No haste, sir, I do know your valor well,   25
Since you durst publish what you are, sir.

Corv.   Tarry,
I'ld speak with you.

Volp.   Sir, sir, another time—

Corv. Nay, now.   30

Volp.   O God, sir! I were a wise man,
Would stand the fury of a distracted cuckold.

      Mosca walks by them.

Corb. What, come again!

Volp.   Upon 'em, Mosca; save me.

Corb. The air's infected where he breathes.   35

Corv.   Let's fly him.

[*Exeunt Corvino and Corbaccio.*]

Volp. Excellent basilisk! Turn upon the vulture.

[*Enter Voltore.*]

Volt. Well, flesh fly, it is summer with you now;
Your winter will come on.
 Mosca.   Good advocate,   40
Pray thee not rail, nor threaten out of place thus;
Thou'lt make a solecism, as Madam says.
Get you a biggin more; your brain breaks loose. [*Exit.*]
 Volt. Well, sir.
 Volp.   Would you ha' me beat the insolent 45
 slave?
Throw dirt upon his first good clothes?
 Volt.   This same
Is doubtless some familiar!
 Volp.   Sir, the court,   50
In troth, stays for you. I am mad a mule
That never read Justinian should get up
And ride an advocate. Had you no quirk
To avoid gullage, sir, by such a creature?
I hope you do but jest; he has not done 't; 55
This 's but confederacy to blind the rest.
You are the heir?
 Volt.   A strange, officious,
Troublesome knave! Thou dost torment me.
 Volp.   I know— 60
It cannot be, sir, that you should be cozened;
'Tis not within the wit of man to do it.
You are so wise, so prudent; and 'tis fit
That wealth and wisdom still should go together.
            [*Exeunt.*]

---

37. BASILISK: legendary serpent with a deadly glance.
43. BIGGIN: cloth skullcap, commonly worn by lawyers.
49. FAMILIAR: attendant demon.
53. QUIRK: knack.

(V.vi.)
25. CONSTANT: composed.

Scene [VI]

[*Enter Four Avocatori, Notario, Bonario, Celia,
Corbaccio, Corvino, Commandadori, etc.*]

1. Avo. Are all the parties here?
Not.   All but the advocate.
2. Avo. And here he comes.

[*Enter Voltore and Volpone.*]

1. Avo. Then bring 'em forth to sentence.
Volt. O my most honored fathers, let your mercy   5
Once win upon your justice, to forgive—
I am distracted—
   Volp. [*Aside*] What will he do now?
   Volt.   O,
I know not which t' address myself to first;   10
Whether your fatherhoods, or these innocents—
   Corv. [*Aside*] Will he betray himself?
   Volt.   Whom equally
I have abused, out of most covetous ends—
   Corv. The man is mad!   15
   Corb.   What's that?
   Corv.   He is possessed.
   Volt. For which, now struck in conscience, here I
    prostrate
Myself at your offended feet, for pardon.   20
   1., 2. Avo. Arise.
   Celia.   O heav'n, how just thou art!
   Volp. [*Aside*]   I'm caught
I' mine own noose—
   Corv. [*Aside to Corbaccio*] Be constant, sir; nought   25
    now
Can help but impudence.
   1. Avo.   Speak forward.

Com.   Silence!
Volt. It is not passion in me, reverend fathers,   30
But only conscience, conscience, my good sires,
That makes me now tell truth. That parasite,
That knave, hath been the instrument of all.
  1. Avo. Where is that knave? Fetch him.
Volp.   I go. [*Exit.*] 35
  Corv.   Grave fathers,
This man's distracted; he confessed it now.
For, hoping to be old Volpone's heir,
Who now is dead—
  3. Avo.   How?   40
  2. Avo.   Is Volpone dead?
  Corv. Dead since, grave fathers—
  Bon.   O sure vengeance!
  1. Avo.   Stay,
Then he was no deceiver?   45
  Volt.   O, no, none;
The parasite, grave fathers.
  Corv.   He does speak
Out of mere envy, 'cause the servant's made
The thing he gaped for. Please your fatherhoods,   50
This is the truth; though I'll not justify
The other, but he may be somedeal faulty.
  Volt. Ay, to your hopes, as well as mine, Corvino.
But I'll use modesty. Pleaseth your wisdoms
To view these certain notes and but confer them,   55
As I hope favor, they shall speak clear truth.
  Corv. The Devil has entered him!
  Bon.   Or bides in you.
  4. Avo. We have done ill by a public officer
To send for him, if he be heir.   60
  2. Avo.   For whom?
  4. Avo. Him that they call the parasite.

---

30. PASSION: anger.
54. MODESTY: moderation.
55. CERTAIN: not to be doubted; CONFER: compare.
82. POSSESSED: i.e., by demons.

3. *Avo.*   'Tis true,
He is a man of great estate now left.
    4. *Avo.* Go you and learn his name, and say the court   65
Entreats his presence here but to the clearing
Of some few doubts.   [*Exit Notario.*]
    2. *Avo.* This same's a labyrinth!
    1. *Avo.* Stand you unto your first report?
Corv.   My state,   70
My life, my fame—
    Bon.   Where is't?
    Corv.   Are at the stake.
    1. *Avo.* Is yours so too?
    Corb.   The advocate's a knave,   75
And has a forked tongue—
    2. *Avo.*   Speak to the point.
    Corb. So is the parasite too.
    1. *Avo.*   This is confusion.
    Volt. I do beseech your fatherhoods, read but those—   80
    Corv. And credit nothing the false spirit hath writ.
It cannot be but he is possessed, grave fathers.
                              [*Exeunt.*]

Scene [VII]

[*Enter Volpone.*]

Volp. To make a snare for mine own neck! And run
My head into it willfully, with laughter!
When I had newly 'scaped, was free and clear!
Out of mere wantonness! O, the dull devil
Was in this brain of mine when I devised it,   5
And Mosca gave it second; he must now
Help to sear up this vein or we bleed **dead.**

[*Enter Nano, Androgyno, and Castrone.*]

How now! Who let you loose? Whither go you now?
What, to buy gingerbread, or to drown kitlings?
 Nano. Sir, Master Mosca called us out of doors, 10
And bid us all go play, and took the keys.
 And.   Yes.
 Volp. Did Master Mosca take the keys? Why, so!
I am farther in. These are my fine conceits!
I must be merry, with a mischief to me! 15
What a vile wretch was I that could not bear
My fortune soberly. I must ha' my crotchets
And my conundrums!—Well, go you and seek him.
His meaning may be truer than my fear.
Bid him he straight come to me to the court; 20
Thither will I, and, if't be possible,
Unscrew my advocate, upon new hopes.
When I provoked him, then I lost myself.

           [Exeunt.]

Scene [VIII]

*[Enter Four Avocatori, Notario, Bonario, Celia,
 Corbaccio, Corvino, etc., as before.]*

 1. Avo. These things can ne'er be reconciled. He
  here
Professeth that the gentleman was wronged,
And that the gentlewoman was brought thither,
Forced by her husband, and there left. 5
 Volt.   Most true.
 Celia. How ready is heav'n to those that pray!
 1. Avo.   But that

(V.vii.)
9. KITLINGS: kittens.
14. CONCEITS: contrivances.
19. TRUER . . . FEAR: more honest than I suspect.
22. UNSCREW: take off the thumbscrew; cease his torture.

(V.viii.)
13. OBSESSION: activation by the Devil through external prompting
rather than by possession.
37. MAKE . . . GOOD: confirm it.

Volpone would have ravished her, he holds
Utterly false, knowing his impotence.   10
   Corv. Grave fathers, he is possessed; again, I say,
Possessed. Nay, if there be possession and
Obsession, he has both.
   3. Avo.   Here comes our officer.

                [*Enter Volpone.*]

   Volp. The parasite will straight be here, grave fa-   15
     thers.
   4. Avo. You might invent some other name, sir var-
     let.
   3. Avo. Did not the notary meet him?
   Volp.   Not that I know.   20
   4. Avo. His coming will clear all.
   2. Avo.   Yet it is misty.
   Volt. May't please your fatherhoods—
   Volp. [*Whispers to Voltore*] Sir, the parasite
Willed me to tell you that his master lives;   25
That you are still the man; your hopes the same;
And this was only a jest—
   Volt.   How?
   Volp.   Sir, to try
If you were firm and how you stood affected.   30
   Volt. Art sure he lives?
   Volp.   Do I live, sir?
   Volt.   O me!
I was too violent.
   Volp.   Sir, you may redeem it: 35
They said you were possessed; fall down and seem so.
I'll help to make it good. (*Voltore falls.*) God bless
     the man!
[*Aside to Voltore*] Stop your wind hard and swell—
     See, see, see, see!   40
He vomits crooked pins! His eyes are set,
Like a dead hare's hung in a poulter's shop!

His mouth's running away! Do you see, signor?
Now 'tis in his belly.

   Corv.   Ay, the Devil!   45

   Volp. Now in his throat.

   Corv.   Ay, I perceive it plain.

   Volp. 'Twill out, 'twill out! Stand clear. See where
     it flies,

In shape of a blue toad with a bat's wings!   50
Do not you see it, sir?

   Corb.   What? I think I do.

   Corv. 'Tis too manifest.

   Volp.   Look! He comes t' himself!

   Volt. Where am I?   55

   Volp. Take good heart, the worst is past, sir.
You are dispossessed.

   1. Avo. What accident is this?

   2. Avo. Sudden, and full of wonder!

   3. Avo.   If he were   60
Possessed, as it appears, all this is nothing.

   Corv. He has been often subject to these fits.

   1. Avo. Show him that writing. Do you know it, sir?

   Volp. [*Aside to Voltore*] Deny it, sir, forswear it,
     know it not.   65

   Volt. Yes, I do know it well, it is my hand;
But all that it contains is false.

   Bon.   O, practice!

   2. Avo. What maze is this!

   1. Avo.   Is he not guilty then,   70
Whom you there name the parasite?

   Volt.   Grave fathers,
No more than his good patron, old Volpone.

   4. Avo. Why, he is dead.

---

43. RUNNING AWAY: contorted.
68. PRACTICE: trickery.
86. PROPER: handsome.
89. WAY: admittance.
101. QUICK: alive.

Volt.   O, no, my honored fathers,   75
He lives—
   1. Avo. How! Lives?
   Volt.   Lives.
   2. Avo.   This is subtler yet!
   3. Avo. You said he was dead.   80
   Volt.   Never.
   3. Avo.   You said so.
   Corv.   I heard so.
   4. Avo. Here comes the gentleman; make him way.
   3. Avo. A stool!   85

[*Enter Mosca.*]

   4. Avo. [*Aside*] A proper man and, were Volpone
      dead,
A fit match for my daughter.
   3. Avo.   Give him way.
   Volp. [*Aside to Mosca*] Mosca, I was almost lost; 90
      the advocate
Had betrayed all; but now it is recovered.
All's o' the hinge again—Say I am living.
   Mosca. What busy knave is this? Most reverend
      fathers,   95
I sooner had attended your grave pleasures,
But that my order for the funeral
Of my dear patron did require me—
   Volp. [*Aside*]   Mosca!
   Mosca. Whom I intend to bury like a gentleman.   100
   Volp. [*Aside*] Ay, quick, and cozen me of all.
   2. Avo.   Still stranger!
More intricate!
   1. Avo. And come about again!
   4. Avo. [*Aside*] It is a match, my daughter is   105
      bestowed.
   Mosca. [*Aside to Volpone*] Will you gi' me half?
   Volp.   First I'll be hanged.

Mosca.   I know
Your voice is good, cry not so loud.   110
  1. Avo.   Demand
The advocate. Sir, did not you affirm
Volpone was alive?
  Volp.   Yes, and he is;
This gent'man told me so. [*Aside to Mosca*] Thou 115
    shalt have half.
  Mosca. Whose drunkard is this same? Speak, some
    that know him.
I never saw his face. [*Aside to Volpone*] I cannot now
Afford it you so cheap.   120
  Volp.   No?
  1. Avo.   What say you?
  Volt. The officer told me.
  Volp.   I did, grave fathers,
And will maintain he lives with mine own life,   125
And that this creature told me. [*Aside*] I was born
With all good stars my enemies.
  Mosca.   Most grave fathers,
If such an insolence as this must pass
Upon me, I am silent; 'twas not this   130
For which you sent, I hope.
  2. Avo.   Take him away.
  Volp. Mosca!
  3. Avo.   Let him be whipped.
  Volp.   Wilt thou betray me? 135
Cozen me?
  3. Avo. And taught to bear himself
Toward a person of his rank.
  4. Avo. Away.   [*The officers seize Volpone.*]
  Mosca. I humbly thank your fatherhoods.   140
  Volp. [*Aside*]   Soft, soft. Whipped!

---

111. DEMAND: question.
157. CHIMERA: mythical monster combining characteristics of a
lion, a goat, and a dragon.

And lose all that I have! If I confess,
It cannot be much more.

    4. Avo.   Sir, are you married?

    Volp. They'll be allied anon; I must be resolute: 145
The fox shall here uncase.   *He puts off his disguise.*

    Mosca.   Patron!

    Volp.   Nay, now
My ruins shall not come alone; your match
I'll hinder sure; my substance shall not glue you   150
Nor screw you into a family.

    Mosca.   Why, patron!

    Volp. I am Volpone, and this [*Points to Mosca*] is
    my knave;
This, [*To Voltore*] his own knave; this, [*To Corbaccio*] 155
    avarice's fool;
This, [*To Corvino*] a chimera of wittol, fool, and
    knave.
And, reverend fathers, since we all can hope
Nought but a sentence, let's not now despair it.   160
You hear me brief.

    Corv.   May it please your fatherhoods—

    Com.   Silence!

    1. Avo. The knot is now undone by miracle.

    2. Avo. Nothing can be more clear.   165

    3. Avo.   Or can more prove
These innocent.

    1. Avo. Give 'em their liberty.

    Bon. Heaven could not long let such gross crimes be
    hid.   170

    2. Avo. If this be held the highway to get riches,
May I be poor!

    3. Avo. This's not the gain, but torment.

    1. Avo. These possess wealth, as sick men possess
    fevers,   175
Which trulier may be said to possess them.

    2. Avo. Disrobe that parasite.

    Corv., Mosca.   Most honored fathers—

1. Avo. Can you plead aught to stay the course of
    justice?   180
If you can, speak.

    Corv., Volt.   We beg favor.

    Celia.   And mercy.

    1. Avo. You hurt your innocence, suing for the guilty.
Stand forth; and first the parasite. You appear   185
T' have been the chiefest minister, if not plotter,
In all these lewd impostures; and now, lastly,
Have with your impudence abused the court
And habit of a gentleman of Venice,
Being a fellow of no birth or blood;   190
For which our sentence is, first thou be whipped;
Then live perpetual prisoner in our galleys.

    Volp. I thank you for him.

    Mosca.   Bane to thy wolfish nature!

    1. Avo. Deliver him to the *Saffi.* [*Mosca is carried* 195
    out.] Thou, Volpone,
By blood and rank a gentleman, canst not fall
Under like censure; but our judgment on thee
Is that thy substance all be straight confiscate
To the hospital of the *incurabili.*   200
And since the most was gotten by imposture,
By feigning lame, gout, palsy, and such diseases,
Thou art to lie in prison, cramped with irons,
Till thou beest sick and lame indeed. Remove him.

    Volp. This is called mortifying of a fox.   205

    1. Avo. Thou, Voltore, to take away the scandal
Thou hast giv'n all worthy men of thy profession,
Art banished from their fellowship and our state.
Corbaccio, bring him near! We here possess
Thy son of all thy state and confine thee   210
To the monastery of San Spirito;

---

205. MORTIFYING: a culinary method of tenderizing meat.
221. BERLINO: pillory.
240. FACT: crime.

Where, since thou knewst not how to live well here,
Thou shalt be learned to die well.
 Corb.   Ha! What said he?
 Com. You shall know anon, sir.   215
 1. Avo.   Thou, Corvino, shalt
Be straight embarked from thine own house and rowed
Round about Venice, through the Grand Canal,
Wearing a cap with fair long ass's ears
Instead of horns; and so to mount, a paper 220
Pinned on thy breast, to the *berlino*—
 Corv.   Yes,
And have mine eyes beat out with stinking fish,
Bruised fruit, and rotten eggs—'Tis well. I'm glad
I shall not see my shame yet.   225
 1. Avo.   And to expiate
Thy wrongs done to thy wife, thou art to send her
Home to her father, with her dowry trebled.
And these are all your judgments.
 All.   Honored fathers. 230
 1. Avo. Which may not be revoked. Now you begin,
When crimes are done and past and to be punished,
To think what your crimes are. Away with them.
Let all that see these vices thus rewarded
Take heart and love to study 'em. Mischiefs feed 235
Like beasts, till they be fat, and then they bleed.
          [*Exeunt.*]

    [*Volpone comes forward.*]

 Volp. The seasoning of a play is the applause.
Now, though the fox be punished by the laws,
He yet doth hope there is no suff'ring due
For any fact which he hath done 'gainst you. 240
If there be, censure him; here he doubtful stands.
If not, fare jovially and clap your hands.
          [*Exit.*]

References for Further Reading

Jonson's *Volpone* appears in many collections of English drama. The best critical edition of Jonson's works is that by C. H. Herford and Percy Simpson (11 vols., Oxford, 1925-52). The most recent edition of *Volpone* is by Alvin B. Kernan for "The Yale Ben Jonson." (New Haven, 1962). Information about Jonson the playwright is also available in the commentary in the Herford and Simpson edition and in the following books: Jonas H. Barish, *Ben Jonson and the Language of Prose Comedy* (Cambridge, Mass., 1960); Gerald E. Bentley, *Shakespeare and Jonson: Their Reputations in the Seventeenth Century Compared* (2 vols., Chicago, 1945); Marchette Chute, *Ben Jonson of Westminster* (New York, 1953; Dutton Everyman Paperback, 1960); John J. Enck, *Jonson and the Comic Truth* (Madison, 1957); James T. Foard, *The Dramatic Dissensions of Jonson, Marston, and Dekker* (London, [1897?]); L. C. Knights, *Drama and Society in the Age of Jonson* (London, 1937); Robert F. Knoll, *Ben Jonson's Plays: An Introduction* (Lincoln, Nebraska, 1964); Robert Gale Noyes, *Ben Jonson on the English Stage, 1660–1776* (Cambridge, Mass., 1935); and John Palmer, *Ben Jonson* (New York, 1934). R. F. Patterson has edited *Ben Jonson's Conversations with William Drummond of Hawthornden* (London, 1923).